Poets at Work

Poets at Work

ESSAYS BASED ON THE MODERN POETRY
COLLECTION AT THE LOCKWOOD MEMORIAL
LIBRARY, UNIVERSITY OF BUFFALO, *by*

RUDOLF ARNHEIM
W. H. AUDEN
KARL SHAPIRO
DONALD A. STAUFFER

Introduction by CHARLES D. ABBOTT

New York
HARCOURT, BRACE AND COMPANY

Contents

List of Illustrations

Foreword

THE MODERN poetry collection of the University of Buffalo is a striking illustration of the germinating forces latent in a creative idea. The idea was Mr. Abbott's and in his introduction to this volume he tells how it was conceived and how it grew. To one who has observed the development of the undertaking from the outside, and only intermittently, its unfolding seems to have had the quality of inevitability. What else, one is tempted to ask, could have been expected? If this question appears to ignore the energy and tenacity with which the project has been pursued by its originator, or the generous and indispensable assistance it has received from hundreds of poets, reviewers, students of literature and lay admirers of the poets' art, such is not the intention. It is merely to acknowledge that "in the beginning was the word," and at the same time to subscribe to Faust's interpretation: "in the beginning was the act."

Although the collection is housed by the University of Buffalo and is legally the University's property, in a wider sense it does not belong to the University. It belongs to the great company of poets now writing in the English language. Their contributions have made it, and particularly their comprehension of the importance of this effort to reveal, however imperfectly, the mysterious and infinitely varied workings of the process of artistic creation. It belongs also—although they may not know it—to the much smaller company of psychologists who are just beginning to try to explain the complex mechanism of esthetic production and the esthetic experience.

It belongs, we hope, to the future, to practicing artists and to students alike who, as time goes on, may find here new bases of understanding and appreciation and new inspiration.

The project cannot be measured by any material yardstick. But no one who has followed its evolution can fail to be impressed by the fact that it has been relatively inexpensive. Indeed, the wonder grows that so much can have been accomplished at so slight a cost. Two grants from the Carnegie Corporation have covered the major part of the direct financial outlay. The University's obligation to that foundation is here once more gratefully acknowledged. Without this assistance at two critical moments the undertaking might well have languished, and perhaps expired. At the same time the opinion may be hazarded that few of the Carnegie Corporation's contributions to the promotion of the arts have brought such rich returns.

The collection is unique, and must remain unique. It is impossible to imagine how it can be duplicated, at least during the present generation. The hundreds of living poets who have built it by contributing their manuscripts and worksheets have in a sense patented it and precluded any imitation elsewhere. This fact imposes upon the University of Buffalo a grave moral responsibility. It is in honor bound to strive unremittingly to approach as closely as possible the unattainable goal of completeness. It is bound also to open this extraordinary treasure house to students and practitioners of the poetic art from all parts of the English-speaking world, and to further their use of it by every device that hospitality may suggest.

This volume represents the first extensive study of the collection by four distinguished writers and scholars who have examined the material from four different points of view. It forms part of the group of contributions to the interpretation of the arts and to the advancement of the sciences which the

University of Buffalo is offering to the public as a memorial of its centenary. The University records its grateful appreciation of the careful and illuminating analysis which each of them has presented.

SAMUEL P. CAPEN, *Chancellor*
University of Buffalo

Acknowledgment

To each poet who has generously allowed his preparatory worksheets to be studied and quoted, the authors of this book wish to express their sincerest gratitude.

Introduction

CHARLES D. ABBOTT

L'Histoire de la Littérature s'est grandement développée de nos jours, et dispose de nombreuses chaires. Il est remarquable, par contraste, que la forme d'activité intellectuelle, qui engendre les œuvres mêmes, soit fort peu étudiée, ou ne le soit qu'accidentellement et avec une précision insuffisante. Il est non moins remarquable que la rigueur qui s'applique à la critique des textes et à leur interprétation philologique se rencontre rarement dans l'analyse des phénomènes positifs de la production et de la consommation des œuvres de l'esprit.

. . . .

Achille ne peut vaincre la tortue s'il songe à l'espace et au temps.

Cependant, il peut arriver au contraire que l'on prenne à cette curiosité un intérêt si vif et qu'on attache une importance si éminente à la suivre, que l'on soit entraîné à considérer avec plus de complaisance, et même avec plus de passion, *l'action qui fait*, que *la chose faite*.

—PAUL VALÉRY

May 3.

46

And
likewise in the (same) hermeneutic of ART
whereof all excellence (as a rare fruit
on the =personality of (some gifted stock) renewing
inborn faculty
Creative Reason is barren; altho'
will collaborate actively & eagerly
with various governance, appear i in some — 740
as happy selection or delay'ed approve
of spiritual nativities, that teem in to mind,
escape, like bubbles, in a pot
when the red fire beneath bristleth, stirreth 750
the water to any ebullience — or in enow
as toilsome exploration of larval germs, wh:
while confidently he labореth thereat
slowly as a modeller in clay. itself
Reason is powerless sheweth when philosophers
will treat of ART, the which are apt to do 75c
having good intuition that their master key
may lie therein:

arch=personalit.

Page from ms. of Book II, *The Testament of Beauty,*
by Robert Bridges.

IT IS now nearly twelve years since the seeds of the "modern poetry collection" were planted in the Lockwood Memorial Library of the University of Buffalo. The collection may now be pronounced "of age." This does not mean that growth is to stop; on the contrary, growth should continue to an even greater luxuriance. The doors are open; the collection is ready for use. This book is an invitation to all who may be interested in twentieth-century poetry. But first, before I tell the story of the collection's making, I should like to describe its diversities, to enumerate the materials out of which it is built.

In rough round numbers—frequent additions preclude arithmetical accuracy—there are at the present time:

(1) 10,000 printed books. First editions of every English-writing poet, any part of whose work was produced in the twentieth century; subsequent editions, if the author has revised the text or added something new (mere reprints are ignored); anthologies, especially those which are compilations of that current poetry which might not, without them, have received publication so early; biographies of poets, memoirs of non-poets if they contain important biographical materials about poets; critical studies both of individuals and of movements; and books of theory, philosophic, psychologic, technical, if they enter the field of that esthetic which underlies or interprets the poetical impulse.

(2) 350 files of magazines. *The Little Review, Others, Broom, The Hound and Horn; The Savoy, Coterie, The Chapbook, New Verse; transition, The Transatlantic Review.* These are examples. They and their many companions, some doggedly persistent, some carelessly ephemeral, have been the daring paratroopers who carried the different, the unex-

3

pected, the dangerous results of poetic experimentation and rebellious thought into enemy country. In their pages first, and often only, appear the harbingers of new methods, of new intent, innovations which may or may not be later assimilated by the body poetic but which, whatever their final disposition, are manifestations of vitality.

(3) 3,000 sets of worksheets. These may be manuscript, typescript, or a mixture of both, depending upon the habits and tastes of the individual poet. They may be bound in serviceable notebooks; they may be loose sheets of paper, torn fragments of copy-book leaves, flaps of used envelopes, backs of gas and electricity bills (paid and unpaid, or at least unreceipted). Some record with remarkable thoroughness the complete history of a poem's making, some present only the later stages of revision, some are fresh and clean and fair, showing nothing at all except the text just as it appears if published. These last are happily a minority. Some poets are represented by only one poem, some by hundreds. There are great and famous names on many, and names almost unknown on others—but who can tell how a future generation will distribute its "greats" and its "obscures"?

(4) 2,500 letters. Many of these have come direct from the poet. They are explanations of his compositional methods or elucidations of his poetic technique. Often they are important complements to the worksheets, occasionally indispensable aids to the penetration of a worksheet's maze of words. And then there are other letters, letters in long series, letters that are the fruit of years of correspondence between poets, or between a poet and his friend, or, as in the case of one notable collection (Robert Bridges to Fuller Maitland and Berkeley Squire), between a poet and specialists in a field kindred to the poet's own. These are of obvious biographical and critical value; they are less revelatory than the worksheets of a poet's

instinctive ways but they provide a useful index to his overt methods and intentions.

Such, in their four main divisions, are the materials out of which is building a kind of laboratory where the study of that "intellectual activity which gives birth to works themselves" may be encouraged, where the scholar, the critic, and the poet as well, may devote himself to "the analysis of the positive phenomena of the production and of the perfecting of [poetic] works of the mind." The building has already taken more than a decade. There is still much to do: elusive books and magazines to be found that embarrassing gaps may be filled; important voices to be persuaded that they should not go unheard among the manuscripts and the letters; the work of newly discovered talents to be added; the representation of some poets, at the moment inadequate, to be strengthened by further examples of their worksheets. There is no end to what remains still to do, since the ideal of completeness will always beckon. That impossible ideal cannot be achieved but it can be stoically sought. Along the way there have been and will be failures; only out of the successes can the laboratory grow, surely and steadily, into a greater and greater usefulness, giving its services to all who seek them.

This volume is, so to speak, the laboratory's public dedication, its formal offer of hospitality to those who are willing to approach the problems of twentieth-century poetry seriously. Four experts—a literary scholar, a psychological esthetician, and two poets, one American, the other, until recently, an Englishman—have been asked to explore and to assess the laboratory's offerings; to suggest how they may be best used, to what ends of research and investigation they may contribute; to show by example or by comment what they imply, what they mean. This volume belongs to the experts, to say what they will; but before its pages are turned over to them, it is necessary to explain how the laboratory came to be, what ideas lay behind its origin, how it grew through chance and choice. The findings of the experts will be all the clearer for that introduction.

I

The "poetry project," as we have come to call it, was not conceived all at once. It grew like one of those houses which start with a single room and gradually receive others as the needs of the family or the ambitions of the owner expand. The first room was born of a hunch.

It was 1935. The University had just acquired a handsome, spacious, and well-equipped library, the gift of Mr. Thomas B. Lockwood. As its newly appointed librarian, I had come before its policies were formulated, its habits and methods developed. It had no past interlaced with traditions which the present must honor. Now the primary duty of a university librarian is obvious enough. It is his function to provide, within the resources of his budget, everything that the faculty and students require for their work. It is no infringement of the creed to envisage future wants, so long as you do not neglect those that are immediate. Moreover, if there is inherent reason at their base, future wants can be bred. But what future wants? There you have got to make a choice. However great your capital resources—and ours were very slim indeed—you cannot build for all fancied future demands, and do the job well, with absolute thoroughness, with a completeness that omits nothing. This kind of downright masterbuilding compels a strict specialization. It requires love, a purposed and resolute attachment that will not diminish in strength, however long and slow the period of construction. The choice, therefore, is of supreme importance.

What could I love with a strength like that? with a constancy that no failure could embitter, no opposition disrupt? something the delights of which could never wane? The answer was poetry. But poetry is an enormous, endless abstraction. It begins with the Hebrews and the Greeks and has three thousand years of uninterrupted flowing. I would have to be more concrete, more limited, than that. To collect, in the totality I was contemplating, the poetry of the Elizabethans, the Augustans, or the Romantics, would entail an investment quite beyond our means, and besides, that had been done magnificently in many another library. But modern poetry? On the scale I had in mind, we could hardly afford even that. But it was not ruinously impractical. We could start, and with method and patience we might establish, little by little, just such an edifice as my hunch was prompting.

It was October 1935. Modern poetry it was to be. The first order went out for books: T. S. Eliot, Robert Frost, Edith Sitwell, Elinor Wylie, W. B. Yeats, whatever appeared in the booksellers' lists at considerate prices. The financial limitation was severe. The librarian's creed and the necessity of filling immediate wants of faculty and students made it unethical to spend the University's money. Small funds could be raised, however, through an organization of the library's friends. They were enough for a modest beginning. We would endeavor to build, piece by piece, a collection of books which would include every text by a twentieth-century poet writing in English. We would get every edition that recorded authentic variants. And we would keep constantly in front of us the goal of completeness, that desert mirage, forever vanishing to reappear in the distance. In this one field, we would construct a bibliographer's paradise and, what is more important, provide the textual and interpretative scholar of later generations with what his counterpart of today can seldom consult in one library: the whole sequential body of a poet's printed work. Whoever the Wordsworth or the Coleridge of our age may turn out to be, his de Selincourt or Lowes may hope to find on our shelves the sources for his study.

II

It is inspiriting even now to remember those early months: the heady explorations of lists and catalogues, the expeditions to local shops, the book-packets pouring in, the tense excitement of discovering what had been captured and what had been lost to another, earlier, claimant. It is astonishing that so much was accomplished out of so lean a purse. Nuggets like *A Shropshire Lad* and *Songs of Childhood* were beyond reach; they belonged to the world of gilt-edged securities. But many a good poet had not brushed the skirts of fashion, had not stimulated the taste of the wealthy connoisseur whose kiss sends market-values soaring. Charles Montagu Doughty came through almost entire, without, to be sure, the wonderful *Travels in Arabia Deserta* which, though prose, is no adscititious garnish to his verse. Lascelles Abercrombie, Edmund Blunden, Roy Campbell; Alfred Kreymborg, William Rose Benét, Marianne Moore. And the younger poets, Auden and Spender, Fearing and Gregory. They were still in their printed infancy; you could get first editions straight from the publishers, without a collector's bonus. In each case one or two items might be beyond our capacities, but those could wait for better days.

There were perplexing decisions to make. Who was a poet? Whom should we include? Mostly the choices were unmistakable, but the booksellers' lists and the shops' shelves were full of hundreds of names that carried no familiar associations, conveying no message of identity. Among them, perhaps, were voices whose quality, as yet unrecognized, might some day be perceived as cardinal. Any such would be few in number; the bulk would be that tragic phenomenon in this tradesman's world, the untalented aspirant to literary honors caught in the racket of paid-in-advance publication. Many a conscientious schoolteacher or honest bank-teller has relieved the drab round of life with flights of meter, correct or incorrect—an avocation eminently harmless, until the itch for admiration leads to a publisher who sees profits ahead, profits not from sales but straight from the author's pocket. These are not poets and the touchstone of print cannot change them into poets. The only reasonably safe criterion for inclusion was the imprint of a reliable publisher, one whom common knowledge accepts as above the deceits of promotional chicanery, whose name is sign that this book is a legitimate contribution to the poetry of its time. Exceptions could be made later, when necessary. More than one respected poet has started his career with a volume released under questionable auspices.

Other problems: What of the occasional poet—the diplomat, the biologist, the financier who publishes a desultory volume of verse? the novelist who turns now and again to poetry but is not seriously a poet? the poet-novelist whose work in two genres it would be invidious to appraise separately? Should the prose as well as the poetry of each individual, whatever his poetic significance, be admitted? Here the answers seem somewhat arbitrary, perhaps capricious. Yes, the occasional poet, often a distinguished person (and, if published at all, almost certainly his book comes from a reputable house), must be included. The very fact that Lord Vansittart and Julian Huxley write verses carries implications that should not be overlooked. On the other hand, since it is doubtful whether antifascist polemics and expository science would afford much aid to the study even of the Vansittart and Huxley poems, their other books may be neglected. But the

occasional poet who is by profession an imaginative writer?
He propounds a more subtle difficulty. John Galsworthy and
Sheila Kaye-Smith, Edith Wharton and Willa Cather, Ernest
Hemingway and William Faulkner have all written and published poetry. In contrast to their other and more established
work, it is casual, often the harvest of their immaturity. But
also it is frequently germinal. It must be represented. But
what about *The Forsyte Saga,* or *Sanctuary,* or *A Farewell
to Arms?* The decision is very hard, because sometimes the
verbal manner of the novel has left its mark on other people's poetry, has given its originator a position of influence
among poets; but the line has to be drawn somewhere in spite
of hesitations. Fortunately such books are universal property
and may be read anywhere, which is not true of *April Twi-
lights* or *A Pushcart at the Curb.* The genuinely indivisible
poet-novelist is another matter. When the texture of prose
and poetry is all of one weaving, when it is impossible to read
one without remembering the other, then there is no debate:
both must stand side by side, *The Memoirs of a Midget* with
Peacock Pie, The Plumed Serpent with *Birds, Beasts and
Flowers, The Venetian Glass Nephew* with *Black Armour.*

It was December 1936. With the poetry collection in mind,
I had been doing lots of reading in the field of prosodic
analysis, of esthetic principle, of textual criticism and interpretation. Many books had imparted their theories: some
conventional, some heretical; some commonplace, some visionary; some scholarly, some impetuous. But nearly all had
one thing in common: they were the verdicts of deductive
reasoning. Seeking to explain the basic origins as well as the
ultimate aims of poetic endeavor (and all the processes of
thought which lie between the beginning and the end), they
started from the finished poem and unwound the ribbon of
conjecture, backwards. They were absorbed in the explication
of causes while their evidence consisted almost wholly of

effects. What Paul Valéry was later to call *l'action qui fait* kindled the invention of each theorist, but the raw materials, the bricks and mortar with which he must build, were nearly always *la chose faite*. The past has not provided what he needed.

Some highly important manuscripts that put forward many a useful clue did exist—a holograph of "Lycidas" before its final consummate polish was applied; remarkable early drafts of Keats's poems; considerable quantities of Wordsworth's *Prelude* in multiple versions; and a handful of others. The majority, however, of manuscripts to survive both the poet's urge to destroy and the housewife's tidiness were "fair copies," differing not at all from the printed lines. One other resource the theorists had at their command and a few had used it well: the revision of a poem's published text in successive editions. James Thomson rewrote *Winter* several times between 1726 and 1748, giving it finally more than double its original length; Mark Akenside did the same, less volubly, with *The Pleasures of the Imagination;* Tennyson had made ruthless changes in his early poems, dictated less by Lockhart's strictures than by his own growing surety of hand. These are but three examples out of the past. Each, and others like them, had been used repeatedly. They were the main props to the theorists' structure. The annals of modern poetry could produce many more. Our methodic accumulation of the poetry project's books would furnish full hampers of this printed material.

Manuscripts. We needed manuscripts if we were to help the scholar in his struggle to penetrate towards the core of the puzzle; if our project were to assist in the pushing back of the barriers that obstruct knowledge; if the beam of light were to be turned full upon *l'action qui fait*. Manuscripts—not "fair copies," not the neat and pretty *simulacra* of a poem in the best-behaved handwriting. Worksheets. That was it. Full worksheets. All the tangible papers that a poet uses in making a poem. Something like that might give the theorist real bricks and mortar. Even if the nebulous inception of a poem could not be captured, the cerebral agitation that precedes the first act of writing, how vividly worksheets might unfold the course of labor, growth and change. The theorist could reason anew, more validly, more confidently, if supplied with adequate evidence. The whole concourse of a poem's worksheets. The past had yielded nothing like that. But they did pose a difficulty, perhaps an insuperable difficulty. Where, how, could we get them?

Worksheets. Every day hundreds were tossed to the wastebasket and the fire. Why not ask for them? Unlike Milton or Keats, most of the poets whose books we collected were alive. To ask could do no harm. At the worst, only rebuffs, a show of tartness or acerbity. But the cheek, the effrontery—asking a poet direct for the formulae of his mint! The insolence of that seemed, at the time, unarguable. The mere thought was enough to shame one into comfortable inactivity. But how else could worksheets ever be got? Without them there was no remotest prospect of moving closer towards the heart of the poem's mystery.

III

The writing of seemly begging letters required circumspection. The poet must not be permitted to believe that we were vastly important, richly endowed, apostolically sanctioned to elicit the secrets of his vineyard. He must be induced to understand that we were young, inexperienced, precariously innocent of authority or license and, at the same time, seriously and utterly sincere. We had an idea far from novel in substance but original in the incidence of its application. He, the poet, held in his own hands the future of the idea's development. By granting our request he could aid in the furthering of an experiment which promised benefits to scholars and critics, perhaps to other poets. Without his active sustenance the idea could only shrivel to inanition.

Letters went forth, fifty in all, to a roster of poets American and British chosen at random from a list of some two hundred, without regard to sex, age, or popularity. The response would determine whether my dreaming had a practical foundation. Each letter asked for a dossier as complete as possible on the composition of a single poem, and invited comments on the general shape of our plans which were explained in as much detail as space would allow. I fear they were dull letters and unreasonably solemn. I know they were long. They had to be, if anything like the full complexity of our design was to be suggested. I had grave doubts of any recipient having the patience to read through the whole of their narrow-margined, single-spaced compactness.

But poets, with some exceptions, are a gracious, indulgent, amenable breed of men. They did read their letters; that is to say, they read parts of their letters. A few may have read but did not acknowledge. A majority sent us what we did not ask for: beautifully immaculate copies of a familiar anthology-piece carefully written in their best calligraphy. Seventeen, however, read the whole of our appeal; approved in principle the objects of the venture; sent, in addition to advice and approbation, genuine worksheets. These seventeen were not at all the least eminent of the fifty. The whole score is important: three complete silences, twenty-five "fair copies," seventeen documentary histories of composition, four promises of same if and when available, and one thunderous rejoinder from Rapallo, a mettlesome volley aimed not at our purposes but at the whole structure of American education.

The seventeen sets of worksheets were not of equal completeness. Several were exactly what we had desired, thorough recordings of the compositional processes; most were variously fragmentary, representing only a few of the stages of evolution. Some were like palimpsests where nothing had been erased; some covered multiple pages through which version succeeded version in ordered sequence; others were sheaves of typescript that resembled in form, though hardly in content, the ancient nursery fable of the old woman, her crooked sixpence, and the pig that wouldn't go over the stile— except that the shifting increments came after instead of before the steady repetitions. Each in its different way revealed something of the ferment that worked towards creation; together they offered what seemed incontrovertible proof that our experiment was not futile, that our nervous hopes were justified.

We wrote to more poets. We tried again the twenty-five who had contributed "fair copies." At times we met blunt hostility. We tested new letters which groped for a sterner brevity of phrase, a less tiresomely expository statement of program. Inevitably, despite all our efforts, more and more "fair copies" arrived, but the numbers of authentic worksheets increased too. Admirable examples came from Louise Bogan, from John Peale Bishop, from Edna St. Vincent Millay, from Christopher Morley. From Rome came a beautifully rubricated notebook on the pages of which an American philosopher, always a poet at heart, had inscribed in the meticulous script of his student and instructorial days at Harvard a cluster of early sonnets—not exactly worksheets, this, yet invaluable because it registered prevenient versions of known poems as well as texts of those unknown. And, most thrilling of all, a collection of materials from Genevieve Taggard so complete, so detailed, so exhaustive, that almost no footprint of the mind was lost in the record; materials that conveyed, like nothing I had ever seen before, the sense of excitement, of agonizing growth, that accompanies invention. With such buttresses as these to support our building we could now be more confident in our petitions. Such dossiers of evidence as we wanted did exist, and poets, if they could spare the time to understand our premises, were willing to give them to us.

We tried still further kinds of begging letter. The amount of correspondence involved, just in sheer physical bulk, was staggering. We were often weeks behind with replies. And the results, while gratifying, were frequently not commensurate to the effort. "Fair copies," like Mr. Edwards' cheerfulness, would keep breaking in. It was soon apparent that to do the job well, we must see the poet, talk with him, explain our present status and justify our hopes, answer his questions, convince him of our intellectual and constructive probity. For this, on any large scale, funds which we did not have were necessary. To test my theories I tried a few visits. They were pleasantly, productively successful; it was a pity that a librarian's personal income would permit so few. Interviews accomplished what letters could only approximate. Somewhere, somehow, we must get financial assistance, if the project were to move ahead into the rivers of active acquisition, not to stagnate in a pool of incessant letter-writing.

The University's Chancellor came to inspect what we had been doing. I had not, up to this time, bothered him with a detailed account of our plans. He knew only that we were engaged in some unorthodox scheme that involved modern poetry. With generous faith in my acumen, he had not peered too closely into my vagaries. But now he came and looked. He examined the Santayana notebook, the Taggard portfolios, the documentary histories of poems by Robert Hillyer, Marianne Moore, John Gould Fletcher and others (by this time there were fifty or sixty proper dossiers). To my great delight he was astonished and unreservedly pleased. From that day on, he has been the poetry project's most co-operative and effective friend. I asked for money and he, as I knew, had none to give. Our University is not one of the nation's wealthy institutions. I wanted to put into operation my theory that further growth depended upon personal visits, interviews with the poets themselves. I wanted to go to England for three months. There, thanks to geographical compactness, I could see scores of poets with a minimum of travel. In three months I could prove or disprove my theory. He listened attentively, sympathetically, and said nothing to discourage my zeal. There was tenacity in the set of his shoulders as he set forth down the library stairs.

It was June 1937. I was at home in the country, mowing a lawn. The telephone rang, long-distance. It was the Chancellor. He was reading me a letter which had just come from President Keppel of the Carnegie Corporation. It was the end of a fiscal year and the cupboards were almost bare but, by diligent scraping, fifteen hundred dollars had been uncovered and would be available for a mission to England. Fifteen hundred dollars was not much for three months in England, with travel both ways and lots of other expenses that are never foreseen—and for two people, since my wife must also go. She had worked with me over every detail of method and organization; she is always a part of the "we" of this narrative. Without her, I could not possibly brave the probable discomfitures that lay ahead—a hundred or so of British poets not all of whom would be graciously willing to hear an American's plea for worksheets. Fifteen hundred dollars was not very much; it would have to be supplemented somehow; but it was nonetheless manna from heaven. We could, said the Chancellor's voice at the other end of a bad connection, go at once if that seemed advisable. It did not seem advisable. There was too much still to be arranged. No, it would have to be winter, some time after Christmas.

IV

One of those bright, clear, crisp dawns that the south coast of England does occasionally have in January. The *Aquitania,* after a gray, stormy passage, was steaming up Southampton-water. Our steward came bustling through the ranks with a telegram—for me. It was an auspicious start to our mission: a courteous welcome from a poet who was asking us to see him early before he left for the Riviera. Perhaps the British species would not be recalcitrant after all.

We found lodgings in Ebury Street, convenient, almost too respectable, and pleasant. They were tiny and homely, a garret just under the eaves with only the slightest touch of a Grub Street *patine,* and they enjoyed a landlady of most punctilious conventionality. She provided excellent meals, and objected only half-heartedly to the crowding of further seats around the little table that nestled between our beds and the desk. The miscellaneity of our guests did puzzle and disturb her, however. What looked like a navvy for lunch, elderly spinsters for tea, and a couple of unmistakable Communists for dinner. She was far from certain that poetry, taken in the large, was a reputable calling. Actors, clergymen, shop-keepers—the poet's vocation may wax in any province; they were a mixture she could not easily digest. Sometimes we could feel the chill of her disapproval seeping in with the winter fog.

But *Punch* came to our rescue. It is remarkable what the accolade, be it never so wry or disparaging, of that thoroughly British, thoroughly respectable, thoroughly canonical magazine can do for you. Evoe had made of his weekly contribution a skit about the library of the future, the library at Buffalo that would house indecipherable worksheets out of whose

chaos the long-suffering investigator would try hopelessly to
construct a fabric of reason. It was a good-natured thrust,
based on one of our less happy begging letters; its ridicule
was broad and not unamiable. Our landlady loved it. Anything that *Punch* can make fun of is not too queer. She began
to understand and would even go so far as to suggest special
foods that visiting poets might appreciate.

The flux of poets in Ebury Street was steady—and then
there were meetings outside as well. Tea at the Reform Club
with Herbert Read. Lunch at the Athenaeum with Evoe
whom playful journalistic baiting did not deter from contributing a manuscript—to the probable later confusion of his
imaginary investigator. Interviews in various hostelries and
clubs and offices, all over London and its suburbs. Hilaire
Belloc and James Stephens, Ruth Pitter and Sylvia Townsend
Warner, W. J. Turner and Richard Church: they were all
affable, cordial, co-operative. Nowhere did we meet that
proud truculence for which the Englishman of the comic
strips is famous. They listened patiently to my story, understood what we wanted, were willing to comply with our request. Some, like Humbert Wolfe, could supply full dossiers
at once; others had never saved such vestigial collections and
could only promise that they would do so with work in progress or yet to come. The fruit of these meetings has ripened
well; no year has passed without the fulfillment of some
friendly agreement made at the Ivy, the Savile Club, or in
Ebury Street. A few still remain to be settled, and they will
be, in time; I have learned that the poet is a man of his
word—though he may, God bless him, occasionally forget and
need a bit of reminding.

Quite often there were trips out of town. A lunch at Taplow
with Walter de la Mare, and wonderful talk of a poet's love
for "words," the shibboleth of his calling. At Brighton a day
of remarkable contrasts: Lord Alfred Douglas, genially fussy,

almost benign in his advancing years, discoursing brightly of Oscar Wilde; and Andrew Young, impressively masculine, with nonconformist dignity accompanying us along the darkening esplanade from his Hove parsonage to our train, while he acknowledged, in simple affection, his poetic debt to our compatriot Robert Frost. An almost tropical interlude on the channel coast of the Isle of Wight with Alfred Noyes. Rambles over the Sussex downs with the Martin Armstrongs, through the East Anglian fens with the Gordon Macleods, among Wiltshire pastures with Brian Guinness. Weekends at Oxford and Cambridge where poets, not always academic in style, are fledged by the dozen; where instructors like Blunden and Abercrombie, Lucas and Quiller-Couch, are poets too. And a week in Dublin, where the voice of Yeats, though he himself was painfully absent dying in the south of France, sounded in echoes of revolt or affirmation. This random chronicle is already too long and, if quadrupled in content, could still enroll only the partial list of those whose help was breathing life into our project. It will be wiser to single out three peculiarly significant episodes for elaboration. In one sense they are all alike since each is the record of an active faith in the future usefulness of the laboratory we were building; yet they are not the same, because each implies a different reason for the aid accorded.

Andrew Young had given us the address of Mrs. Freeman whose husband, the poet, had died in 1929. I wrote her a note suggesting that she have lunch or dinner with us in Ebury Street and received in reply a firm invitation to dine with her in Anerley. I was soon to learn that everything about Mrs. Freeman is beautifully firm, and generous as well: her friendships, her loyalties, and certainly her housekeeping. Anerley is a district of London with which I was not then familiar. I knew only that it was far out on the edge and that it was where de la Mare had once lived. I recall that it was a long ride and that, as usual, I was apprehensive at the prospect of facing the unknown, all the more timid because my exchange of notes with Mrs. Freeman had given little or no inkling of purpose. Anerley was dark and the house forbidding, like one of the ghostly houses in de la Mare's poems. I expected no answer from a hesitant knock on the moonlit door. We waited a second. Somebody was there, after all—Mrs. Freeman, her two daughters, and an odd man or two, guests like ourselves. We sat down to one of those meals that come straight out of Dickens and belie the reproofs of those gourmets who despise English food. With such support, conversation grew easy. A warmth of goodwill spread all about. The daughters were lively, the fellow-guests genial, and Mrs. Freeman briskly attentive. I hardly needed to explain my mission. She had divined it, out of a casual phrase either of mine or Andrew Young's. Her husband had greatly admired an American, Herman Melville; had written a book about him. John Freeman had liked Americans, and whatever there was of his poetic worksheets should be ours. He would approve were he alive. And it gave her a feeling of comfort and rectitude to know that his papers would be preserved and cherished in an American institution; that they might serve to instruct, as he would have wished, other poets and critics. He had been an important man-of-affairs during business hours, but his real life had been lived after those hours, when he could give himself to what he loved. She wanted to be actively loyal to what he had loved. This was spirit, not sentiment. We left the house, no longer ghostly, admiring Mrs. Freeman and possessed of a new friendship which eight years has not weakened. Some days later, one of the daughters brought to Ebury Street a large packet of worksheets and other papers, including the manuscripts of the Melville volume in "The English Men of Letters."

The second episode also presents a widow. We were staying on Boar's Hill with friends who had made arrangements for us to see their neighbor, Mrs. Robert Bridges. It was a day dark with forebodings, the Sunday just after Hitler had marched into Austria. Our hosts and everyone else we met were obsessed with memories of 1914, fearful of a future whose threats were growing louder and clearer. In the morning I had had an appointment with Gilbert Murray. We had walked round and round his garden paths, ostensibly discussing the worksheets of translations. *The Trojan Women* and *The Frogs* did not hold his attention; Austria, Czechoslovakia, Poland, crowded them out. He was disillusioned and bitter. After twenty years of devoted service to the ideal of peace, he, like many another proponent of the League of Nations, was helpless and defeated. On that Sunday morning he knew it, and worksheets were an almost unendurable triviality. Not that he said so; he was as kind and helpful as the gentlemanly scholar always is, but his heart was elsewhere. At last it was time to go to Chilswell House.

There too events had cast monitory shadows. Mrs. Bridges was graciously heedful; her daughter, Elizabeth Daryush, a poet of ascendant distinction, more electric than her mother, asked searching questions. Together they showed us what had survived of the late poet laureate's manuscripts. He had normally destroyed the preparatory stages of his work as soon as they had been incorporated into the finished fabric. It happened, however, that a number of pages of the primary version of *The Testament of Beauty* had been kept. In the magnificent Bridges' hand they were things of beauty, even with the multiplicity of their erasures and corrections. Originally their writing was in pencil; that, after revisions many of which were visible as indentations in the paper, was next inked over, making the first basic draft of the poem; then followed the infinite labors of redaction, taking the form of emendations, deletions and additions, superimposed often in red ink. They were worksheets of inestimable value to our purpose, and I did my best to be persuasive. I even suggested that in America they would be safe from bombings. Mrs. Bridges, however, remembered her husband; she felt that there were statements in his philosophy which implied a fundamental opposition to the theories behind our project. With the dignity of her memories there could be no argument. I could only beg that she think the problem over and decide according to the dictates of her conscience. A few weeks later she wrote me that she had made her difficult decision: it was proper, even necessary perhaps, that her husband be represented in such a collection as ours; she was sending therefore two pages of the original draft and, in facsimile, a third page which I had particularly coveted. The two original pages were superb manifestations of the poet-craftsman at work, but I could see that they revealed sufficiently little of the poet-thinker's progress to satisfy the demands of loyalty. Incidentally, they record, as Professor Stauffer points out, one of the philosophical statements which must have been in Mrs. Bridges' mind. The facsimile was a tracing made, with painstaking accuracy, by Mrs. Bridges herself of the first page of Book I. I had liked it because it included six lines not to be found in the printed text. In the tracing these six lines were omitted. Such delicacy, whatever its effect on our designs, seems to me admirable. Mrs. Bridges won the day and I learned a lesson in humility.

And now the third episode, this time in Ebury Street. Stephen Spender came to lunch. He was young and shy and embarrassed. Under his arm was a large official-looking, businesslike book such as one sees on the clerk's desk of an old-fashioned hotel. We gave him sherry and there was no small talk at all. An immediate plunge into the facts. I've got just what you want, he said, proffering the work-a-day, functional

volume. I was reading it on my way; it's pretty good. And it was—a great deal more than pretty good. It contained nearly all the poems of his 1933 collection, one of the significant poetic achievements of the decade. Each poem was there in a completeness that staggered the eye: version after version, false starts and blind alleys, phrases groping for content, metrical filings, images jostling each other in the rush towards finality. It was experience just to examine it, an irresistible absorption into the processes of imaginative creation. It was the real right thing, without any qualifications—perhaps the nearest possible approach to the fury and the pain of "making." And Spender knew we were pleased. Our landlady's buxom little maids brought in the lunch. Somebody had to use a bed for chair, and it was difficult to squeeze Spender's long legs into the cramped space. What had seemed shyness and awkwardness disappeared—and we were all at home, talking enthusiastically about the future of poetry, about what scholars and critics and poets and certainly psychologists might uncover of the mysteries of thought, what those findings might, in turn, give to another generation of poets. It was wild talk, young, and probably irrational, but it was fresh and moving and hopeful.

I shall refer again to these three episodes. They are like fables that illustrate homely truths; only, this time, it is not truths but attitudes of mind that are adumbrated—attitudes of mind that are basic influences upon a project like ours, perhaps upon every culturable enterprise of this queer new world we live in, this new world which wants so passionately to understand *l'action qui fait.*

Our three months in England were over. If there had been any doubts about the superiority of the interview method over the begging-letter approach, they were long since dispelled. We were heartened but tired. Two or three (some-

times as many as five) poets a day are undeniably taxing. The *Aquitania*, even third-class, without a single poet on board, was a blissful harbor of rest on a mild April ocean.

V

During the next year work was lamentably static, a return to the pedestrian gaits that preceded the transatlantic sprint. The dull pressure of finance, or rather the lack of it, kept us soberly quiescent. There was a welter of fairly ineffectual letter-writing, and some progress was made in the accumulation of the less expensive books and periodicals. In general, however, it was a period of torpor, not wholly without value. It was, for example, increasingly evident that patience must be our primary virtue, that we must never try to hurry a poet into compliance. The aftermath of the English trip, its slow but solid late returns, was teaching us that. And it was clear that our first notion of one poem in its complete manuscripts from each poet was more appropriate to a museum than to the kind of laboratory we had gradually come to envisage. The really proficient searcher, whether his intent be the individual poet's achievements or the principles of poetic theory, would need more than one example. In fact, the more he could have in hand, the more valid his conclusions. We must attempt to have every poet represented by a budget of poems, preferably from all the seasons of his accomplishment. The Conrad Aiken of *Earth Triumphant* was hardly the poet of *Brownstone Eclogues*. This would be difficult, in many cases impossible; we could only try. Meanwhile we waited, hoping that the Chancellor's ministrations in our behalf, those prosaic necessary feats of resourceful legerdemain, would permit us to proceed.

It was April 1939. The lights had switched; the prohibitive

red blinked out, an explicit green shone clear. The Chancellor's efforts had availed. Once again the Carnegie Corporation had given us a lift, this time with a grant that cautious management could make do for three or four years. The acquiring of books and little magazines could be more energetic and need no longer be continually checked in the pursuit of some elusive item. The indispensable interviews could begin again and could now be conducted in America on a more leisurely, less strenuous schedule than had ever been possible in England. There was an immediate upsurge of work: new book-buying programs, new letter-writing, long-range planning for essential meetings. Mary Barnard, a poet of impressive promise, came to assist. As curator of the poetry collection, she left her mark in its growth—four permanent and substantially thick tree-rings, like those in the cross-section of a Mesa Verde beam, each the product of a fertile year, before she left us to devote her talents wholly to writing.

The quest for books was now active. At last the hitherto forbidden fruits were often within reach. The gaps in our shelves began to fill. *A Shropshire Lad* joined the less pecuniarily valuable Housmans; *Songs of Childhood* took its rightful place at the head of the de la Mares. *Salt-Water Ballads*, *The Soul's Destroyer*, *Chamber Music* were quickly found. And the early British-printed Robert Frosts. Even such rarities as *The Torrent and the Night Before* and *Flagons and Apples* and *Nets to Catch the Wind*. But the real triumphs of our agent-friends were the ferreting-out of such almost mythical volumes as Yeats's *Mosada*, Pound's *A Lume Spento*, and Sandburg's *In Reckless Ecstasy*. We do not share, and never expect to imitate, the professional collector's worship of "condition." Mint copies, bindings that no finger has ever touched, pages unsullied by the human eye, are fair game for the connoisseur; we do not shoot in the same field. Our books are for use, not, to be sure, for the steady pawing of the uninitiated but for the studied employment of qualified adepts. However tender and reverent the handling, no "mint copy" under usage can long retain its purity. We are satisfied with what the booksellers call a "sound" copy, reasonably clean and still sturdy in its binding. For this, be it happily admitted, we do not have to pay (and could not) the ringing price of the auction-room.

And now interviewing began again, without the rush and repletion of those months in London. Boston and Chicago, Washington and Philadelphia, wherever there were poets we endeavored to find them. New York, of course, was the happiest hunting-ground. There they congregate in numbers almost beyond belief, as they do in London—and for a very simple, though highly deplorable, reason. Very few poets, however able, can make a living out of their craft alone. They have to teach school, or conjure up advertising tricks for an agency, or edit magazines, or review books, or write novels and popular articles, or perform any one of a hundred tasks that the world appreciates more than it does poetry. At least it pays more for them. There is greater opportunity to do these things in a city; in truth many of them it is impossible to do elsewhere. And the larger the city, the more varied the choice of pot-boiling faggots. New York is inevitably full of poets. Perhaps this cruel necessity prevailed equally in other ages, in Athens and Rome and Florence; if so, it is no credit to their civilizations, as it is none to ours. I have been led into a recusant digression for which I am not sorry. I shall have even more protests to add thereto a little later. I like, admire, and respect poets generally, and I find it humiliating to be forced to recognize that few of them ever receive a just return for their services.

I have seen at one time or another nearly every poet in New York and its environs. I became, to use Louis Untermeyer's (I hope affectionate) description, "the well-known manuscript ghoul." Almost without exception each poet has been kind, co-operative, and quick with useful suggestion, in spite of what must often have seemed a pest-like assiduity on my part. Some, like William Carlos Williams and William Rose Benét, perfunctory at first, have given their assistance with such growing goodwill that the whole project has been warmed into new confidence by their faith. From Boston and Chicago and other centers has come similarly cordial aid, so varied, so valuable, so constant, that I am chagrined at my inability, for lack of space and for fear of producing a tedious catalogue of superlatives, to pay tribute where tribute ought honorably to go.

The same concern would hold for the scores of poets who are not city-cloistered, whom we have met in a series of motor-jauntings that carried us into most of the states. Even so, we have missed some, to our sorrow and loss. But we did not miss Leonard Bacon in the manorial seclusion of Peace Dale, or Robinson Jeffers and his rock-built tower that fronts the Pacific, or Paul Engle in the endless corn-fields of Iowa, or Witter Bynner adobe-housed at Sante Fe, or Yvor Winters and Janet Lewis contentedly raising children and goats on the outskirts of Palo Alto, or Sister Mary Madeleva supervising the feminine half of the football paradise Notre Dame. I promised no lists and one has grown, regardless. Let me end it with Louis Untermeyer punning extravagantly in a cool fastness of the Adirondacks. It was he who charted a new journey and provided the rousing stirrup-cup.

He liked our dossiers of worksheets, their revelations of insight and purpose. He had marveled at the seemingly wayward, yet always progressive rewritings of Kenneth Fearing's "American Rhapsody IV" which he had examined once on a visit to the library. It alone, he said, justified our undertaking. But were there not complements to these collections? Other documents that had their uses? What of the letters poets

write and receive among themselves? Are they not full of
biographical detail and critical judgment which would yield
clues quite serviceable to our hypothetical future investigator?
Why not come to Stony Water where he could show exactly
what he meant? Naturally we did not decline—there we received, in a broken-lidded green strong-box, all of the letters
written to the nimblest of anthologists by Sara Teasdale,
Vachel Lindsay, and Amy Lowell.

VI

Louis Untermeyer, seductively open-handed on his moun-
tain-top, brings the narrative portion of this introduction to its
close. That was July 1941. Shortly thereafter war was to disrupt our settled program. I do not mean we forgot or willfully
neglected, during that four-year anguish, our commitments
to a purpose which war could mutilate but not destroy. We
did all we could. Communication was difficult, if not impossible; the younger poets were under arms or serving in some
necessary civilian capacity. The University bulged with sol-
diers whose library needs required a continuous transformation of routines; to observe the librarian's creed kept me
worse than busy. And, as skies cleared and the end was obvious, we quietly resumed our march. It is warming, though,
even now to remember how, in the darkest days, worksheets
would come through from a prison-camp in Norway, from
lonely Pacific islands, from the deserts of Libya or the sultry
Gold Coast of Africa—from poets whom no upheaval could
deflect from their calling.

This has been a narrative too largely personal. That was
inevitable. It takes that form because the poetry project grew
that way. I can only hope that I have made its history legible
—from hesitant birth, through troubled years of propagation,
to a maturity that can never be complete; that I have im-

plied its permanence, its integral consecration to the cause of knowledge, a special, limited, but pregnant segment of knowledge. Perhaps it is mistaken optimism to expect any clarification of the dark mysteries of the mind. But who is sure? And if there can be no ultimate vision into the secret springs of creative thought, then at least we can learn, from these materials, more than we have known before of the overt techniques of poetic communication.

VII

The objection has been occasionally raised by certain poets that our aims constitute an express invasion not only of personal privacy but also of the essential secrets of art. This is true. It is an objection which has to be admitted and, where a poet feels strongly that the mysteries of his craft are inviolate, we try to explain our contrary belief without importunity. Apart from its personal angle which is purely the individual's problem, the objection is based on the conviction, hallowed by centuries of acceptance, that the work of art in its final form is a sacred monument not to be grazed by irreverent hands. It is complete, whole in itself, unchangeable. It may be admired or contemned, in accordance with the vogue of the hour and the observer's capacity to understand. Critics may wrangle over its perfections or its faults. But it exists, absolute and imperishable. How it came to be, or why, does not matter. In fact, to know would destroy its values. It is impious to pry into the skills, the pains, the velleities that produced it. A work of art is a work of art. There it is—take it or leave it.

Besides, the non-artist with his clumsy fingers can never touch the esoteric center. Robert Bridges, in the worksheet to which I have already referred and which Professor Stauffer is to requote later, puts it thus:

> How in its naked self
> Reason wer powerless showeth when philosophers
> wil treat of Art, the which they are full ready to do,
> having good intuition that their master-key
> may lie therein: but since they must lack vision of Art
> (for elsewise they had been artists, not philosophers)
> they miss the way . . .

There are arcana of thought, of the creative imagination, which are too holy for all but the select. It is significant, however, that Bridges defines the magnetic attraction exerted by these mysteries of art upon what he calls the philosopher, what we may interpret as the man who wants to know how and why. The whole passage, which is too long to print in its entirety, implies an increasing awareness that man is demanding a larger knowledge of the corridors of thought. A privileged intelligence, according to the tenets of his logic, Bridges does not approve this tendency; he merely acknowledges it.

In the essays that follow, Mr. Auden and Professor Arnheim both describe our worksheet-gathering as, in idea, a twentieth-century phenomenon. One sees it as sign of a changing attitude towards the arts, representative of a general selfish interest on the part of the individual in the potentialities of the artist's life; the other as an inevitable product of a new age, the age of psychology, an age in which the processes of thought have come to be a primary concern of humanity. The science itself of psychology is a creation of this concern.

To me it seems very evident that only in this new age could such a project have developed. Only against a background of zealous questing for the mind's devious meanings did it become possible. Preceding ages, accepting without question the work of art as fait accompli, would have seen our activities as repellently inquisitive or amusingly absurd. But the twentieth century is earnestly, passionately absorbed in the pursuit of hows and whys. Its thinkers in every field, its philosophers and scientists, are not content to accept anything, even a work of art, without knowing the reasons for its existence, without at least trying to discover the laws that govern its making, the impulses that give it birth. Thought lies behind every man-made object—poem, painting, sonata; the machine-gun, the tank, the submarine; the garden-hose, the tractor, the Grand Central Station; or the kitchen-stove. Thought (which is often the child of experience) has directed their style, controlled their size, made them useful or beautiful, beneficent or destructive. To know more about Thought, any aspect of Thought, is to approach a knowledge of Reality. Of the generally esthetic aspect Robert Bridges was saying just that, somewhat grudgingly, in *The Testament of Beauty;* of the purely literary aspect, Paul Valéry was stating it more explicitly in the paragraphs I have used as epigraph. For good or bad, we want to know what can be known about Thought. Worksheets of poems, we believe, are an important channel through which that knowledge can come.

They have, of course, their limitations; they cannot provide the footprints of Thought in all its various tracks and runways; they can offer only the literary-esthetic approach— but the empire of poetry is large, its matter incalculable, and, by analogy, what is there revealed may have its meanings elsewhere. We have endeavored to include every possible type, that no avenue may be neglected: serious poetry and comic, light verse and heavy (if it be not invidious to call it that); lyric, narrative, bucolic, dramatic, didactic; religious and profane. Alex Comfort and John Betjeman. Anne Ridler and Stevie Smith. Merrill Moore and Richard Armour. Muriel Rukeyser and Phyllis McGinley. And translation as well, for translation, with its different stresses and pressures, demands from the artist other verbal dexterities, other thought-manipulated inventions. Oliver Elton's *Evgeny Onegin*. Maurice Baring's lyrics from the Russian. Jean Starr Untermeyer's tireless modulations of the rhythms of Hermann Broch's *Der Tod des Virgil*. Henry Drinker's renderings of the words used by Bach and Brahms, where the intent is to make every syllable do its musical as well as its literal duty, a highly exacting art.

Worksheets have mainly been contributed by poets who, because they are themselves a part of the twentieth-century pattern, participate in the contemporary will to know. These poets are, to revert to the three episodes narrated of the English trip, like Spender. They are enthusiastically willing to help towards a better understanding of the principles that regulate the creative imagination. They belong, definitely, to the age of psychology. Almost invariably the young poet who has lived the whole of his life amidst the tensions of twentieth-century striving comprehends without effort the ultimate usefulness of worksheets. Oftentimes he has begun to save them long before knowing that such a project as ours was in the offing—irrefutable testimony to the project's roots in the immediacy of demand. But many poets, whose attitudes of mind were shaped by other influences, who acquired their natural convictions before the age of psychology was so notably in the ascendant, have also contributed. They are like Mrs. Freeman and Mrs. Bridges. Some, not wholly understanding, have had faith in the promise and the hope of a younger generation and have courageously given what might aid in the realization of a vision. Others have understood and have not agreed, have not shared in the vision of possible momentous achievements, but have thought it their duty not to obstruct, have honored an obligation the future enjoins on the past.

VIII

The question is sometimes put: Why does the library not pay for its manuscripts? The basic answer is simple and has been inherent in the story I have just told. There has never been any money with which to pay. There has often not been enough for the project's day-to-day subsistence, never enough for its acquisition of books and other printed materials. The present imposing fullness of its shelves is still not the completeness of which we have dreamed; and what there is is there because every penny has told its tale. Even so, many a book has been an unsolicited gift. But poverty is not the whole answer. If we had at our disposal the gigantic funds that would permit us to pay each poet for his worksheets on any scale not laughable, not insulting to the poet's self-esteem, we should not know how to use them. By what yardstick could we measure values? By what balance could we judge the respective market-weights of a Kipling whose phrases are on every tongue and a Hopkins whose images delight only the initiate? By what alchemy of divination could we determine whose accomplishment merited this sum, whose promise that? And if all could be paid alike, all the hundreds of poets who write in the books and the magazines of each passing current year; if there were available a fund so colossal; would not the popular successful poet, the Kipling, say, of the moment, resent his equalization to the Hopkins who is merely read by friends in manuscript? The true democrat would not, but are there many true democrats? Are not most of us rather humanly cantankerous in respect to such comparisons? It is beside the point to insist that we might prefer Hopkins to Kipling. The goal of the project is the total representation of an era's important poetry; to that, both Kipling and Hopkins are essential.

Our thought has necessarily assumed that, in begging for worksheets, we are asking for something which is, sooner or later, commonly destroyed; that the giving inflicts no financial hardship on the individual. It is true there is a market for the manuscripts of the "collected" poet and, as fashion veers in the winds of taste, any poet may become "collectable." The absorptive powers of that market are limited, however, and few poets are so lean of output as to produce only what can be absorbed. They can probably spare, without pecuniary sacrifice, enough for our purposes. It might even be argued that the more they deposit in permanent safe-keeping, the greater the salability of the residue. These are arguments of the counting-house and I have no love for them. It has been the normal custom, when faced by a demand for payment, simply to withdraw our request. Nothing could be further from our intentions than to have a poet feel that by compliance with our entreaty he is depriving himself and his family of justly earned income. Rather than risk that, we infinitely prefer to beat a sorrowful retreat, without debate and without remorseful memories.

But there is a deeper moral problem in all this. Once or twice an indigent struggling poet has put the question, Will the library pay me for manuscripts? And I have felt guilty—not because we cannot pay, but because the world denies him a satisfactory return for his work. Perhaps he possesses extraordinary gifts; perhaps his whole life is devoted to the fulfillment of what his gifts command, and he produces something the world does not relish, the magazines will not buy, the publishers print solely out of pride or kindness. He may be creating something that is right and honest and true. It may or may not be beautiful, as beauty is commonly understood. It may be merely gay, with a gaiety that will not conform. Or it may be bitter with scorn, a whiplash on flesh insensitive to its fury. It is good, beyond all doubt. We recognize it as good. Our grandchildren may worship it. And the man or woman who makes it, out of toil immeasurable and God-given genius, can starve in a hole for all we care. We are on the skirts of one of the eternal mysteries of art. Villon. Schubert. Kit Smart. Keats. Van Gogh. Whitman. Blake. The list could go on, interminably. The strange and unforgettable vice of every age. And there is no imaginable cure. But when I say No to such a poet, shame wells inside me nonetheless, and I am sick with guilt. Villon would have squandered his guerdon on harlots, Kit Smart on drink; Blake, in all likelihood, would have mislaid his. Such defensive reflections, however true, bring no comfort. The personal conscience withers, while the world's nods, complacently unmoved. Perhaps Mr. Auden, in the final section of the essay that concludes this volume, answers for the poet's. It is a good answer, but it does not lay the ghost for the common man, like me, part and piece of the world's mob.

IX

And now, after this long preamble, I must fulfill what should be the first duty of an introduction and present our guests—Professor Stauffer of Princeton University, Mr. Shapiro of the *Essay on Rime* and many another poem, Professor Arnheim of Sarah Lawrence College, and Mr. Auden of the fresh, unpredictable, and always cogent judgment. They have come to explore the poetry collection's holdings, to point out paths that the hypothetical future investigator may follow to his advantage, to suggest the uses to which such materials may be profitably put. They are busy men with many duties elsewhere, many obligations to their own necessities. They have not been able to spend the months that a full mastery of the many sets of documents would require. They have picked and chosen, glanced at this, sampled that, studied with care whatever seemed immediately pertinent to their purpose. They are the first assessors, as it were, of a new property. Their views are not final; they are tentative, reconnoitering, searching; impressions rather than verdicts. Each of the four has worked independently, without restriction, with only a minimum of direction from me. Yet there is almost no overlapping in their essays—only a somewhat heavy usage of the Spender notebook, but that was inevitable; it is such obvious treasure-trove. Professor Stauffer has brought with him the methods of the literary scholar, the skill and learning of professional research. Mr. Shapiro displays the sensitive discriminations of the poet, seeking out fundamentals. Professor Arnheim is a psychologist systematically explaining the poetic process against the background of his science's present theories. And Mr. Auden, like Mr. Shapiro but in a quite different direction, has rushed to fundamentals, not of poetry alone but of the modern *ethos* in its impact on the poet's vocation. Each, in a sense, is a pioneer. Others, I hope, will follow, inheriting the suggestions of the surveyors, and striking out for themselves along new and different roads.

When they come, these hypothetical future investigators, they will, I trust, be grateful, as I am grateful now, to the hundreds of men and women who are the real makers of our laboratory—the poets to whose generosity, sustaining interest, faith and kindness, we must attribute all that is here. Many have been or will be mentioned by name in this volume; many more have been, not forgotten but, for reasons of space and proportion only, left to another occasion. Someday we will publish a catalogue where every contribution will be properly acknowledged, every free-hearted poet happily recorded. When that day comes, I fervently hope that such a catalogue may not be definitive—that a continuously flowing rivulet of worksheets will demand an endless succession of supplements.

Genesis, or The Poet as Maker

DONALD A. STAUFFER

Of whom vivid air spewes the peculiar honour
That, born of the sun, they travelled towards the sun,

                                         truly
I think continually of those who were great.
Who, from the womb, remembered the soul's history
Through corridors of light where the hours are suns
Endless and singing. Whose lovely ambition
Was that their lips, still touched with fire,
Should tell of the Spirit clothed from head to foot in song.
And who hoarded from the Spring branches
The desires falling across their bodies like blossoms.

What is precious is never to forget
The essential delight of the blood, drawn from ageless springs,
Breaking through rocks in worlds before our earth.
Never to deny its pleasure in the morning simple light
Nor its grave evening demand for love.
Never to allow gradually the traffic to smother
                               flowery
With noise and fog the ~~the~~ of the spirit.

Near the snow, near the sun, in the highest fields
See how these names are fêted by the waving grass
And by the streamers of white cloud
And whispers of wind in the listening sky.
~~The names of those who in this life fought for life~~

Final draft of "I Think Continually . . . ," by Stephen Spender.

No CORRECT procedure for criticizing a work of art exists. Nor is there any example of perfect criticism. Every method or school, along with its qualities, has its obvious limitations, which its opponents are delighted to make even clearer. Take as illustrations the two poles of pure-esthetic criticism and historical criticism. The pure esthetes find beauty in form. They believe that every work of art should be self-consistent. They hold, rightly, that a work of art should be judged *as art* in accordance with its own standards. But in their enthusiasm, some of them press further and maintain that each work of art is not only self-consistent but self-contained. Its sacred autonomy must not be disturbed by the intrusion of such irrelevancies as the poet and his world. The weaknesses of this theory it is almost unfair to dwell on. In practice, art for the sake of art leads by various arid trails of experimentation, or *préciosité*, or formal fireworks, to a final inanition. Its critical defenders are forced to disregard most of the history of art because it seems to them so vulgarly impure.

On the other side, the historical critics insist upon seeing the work of art against its fullest background. Admirable and defensible as their intention is, here also the limited consideration of a single goal can lead rapidly to serious abuse. The work of art may be forgotten in the search for some new fact in the life of its creator, as incontrovertible as it is insignificant. And now that the pure-esthetes have healthily laughed out of existence the question, How many children had Lady Macbeth? it is perhaps equally needless in understanding Shakespeare as an artist to ask, How many children had Anne Hathaway? (Provided, indeed, that we are actually talking about Shakespeare's wife. If her name could be established beyond all cavil, how much additional light would that throw on his plays?) The learned journals of the last half-century have been filled with listings of parallel passages, usually sterile because uninterpreted, comparing some author with another less noted. Articles are written, not only on what some poet or painter read or looked at, but on what he *might* have read or looked at. The game seems to be to demonstrate that a first-rate artist may be explained as a picker and stealer from his second-rate forebears. Analogues, debts, sources, schools, and climates of opinion! To apply Arnold's description of God, a work of art becomes a stream of influence not ourselves that makes for scholarship.

With naïve hopefulness, this essay proposes to marry only the finer strains in these two schools of *l'art pour l'art* and *historismus*. It will assume with the estheticians that the work of art merits our direct attention, and with the historical critics that any work of art must have grown out of *something*. What are its legitimate ancestors? Only what was in the artist's mind in the process of gestation and creation. And on what basis can they be established? Only, if we feel respect for the laws of evidence, on the basis of what the artist himself leaves as record.

The theory is easy to state, hard to apply. The trouble lies in the truth, embarrassing for critics, that although much can be learned of the real significance of a work of art from its process of creation, the artist usually presents to the public merely the finished product. Since the mind of Zeus in the throes of thought is hard to observe, it is much easier to fall into the esthetic heresy that Pallas Athene sprang full-born into the world, but did not spring from anywhere in particular. If only we could follow her *ab ovo*, and note what forces delicately shaped the growing, uncertain organism before its full maturity!

The Lockwood Memorial Library at the University of

Buffalo affords easily the best, and in many respects the only, organized facilities in this country for such genetic criticism. The finished poems are there, in an admirable collection of modern verse running to over 10,000 volumes, not to mention amazingly complete files of the little magazines and ephemeral repositories to which our civilization has consigned so much of its best poetry. More important for the purposes of this essay is its large, varied, and catalogued collection of original manuscripts, variant drafts, and worksheets by contemporary poets. To practicing poets, critics, and amateurs this collection offers unparalleled chances to scrutinize poetry-in-the-making. And since the root meaning of poetry is "to make," perhaps such scrutiny of poetry-in-the-making insures most certainly that one is looking at the thing itself, and not at something off the track.

Because this essay will take the form of "My first acquaintance with the poets" as they have allowed themselves to be preserved in essence in the Lockwood Library, and because it will consider the extraordinary variations that actually occur in the process of building a poem, it might be well to inquire, limiting ourselves to one well-known example, as to what certainty escapes us in interpreting a poem when we lack such resources as are now available at Buffalo. Let me quote entire the last poem in *A Shropshire Lad:*

> I hoed and trenched and weeded,
> And took the flowers to fair:
> I brought them home unheeded;
> The hue was not the wear.
>
> So up and down I sow them
> For lads like me to find,
> When I shall lie below them,
> A dead man out of mind.

Some seed the birds devour,
    And some the season mars,
But here and there will flower
    The solitary stars,

And fields will yearly bear them
    As light-leaved spring comes on,
And luckless lads will wear them
    When I am dead and gone.

Now how would we approach this if we considered it as a self-contained and self-explanatory poem? I must confess that on copying it after not having looked at it for years, I suddenly felt as I finished the second stanza: "But that's the end of the poem!" Perhaps such an instinctive feeling may indicate some flaw in structure. A close reading, however, makes it possible to justify, or rationalize, the whole. One may admire the formal balance between the two halves, or the repetition of the idea of the second stanza in the expansion and variation of the last. One may point out the orderly arrangement of the thought—the statement of a situation in the first two stanzas, and in the last two, the restatement of the situation in a more general context that suggests the Biblical parable of the sower and the seeds.

But Housman himself, in *The Name and Nature of Poetry*, has spoken of its genesis. Two of the stanzas came easily and perfectly as he was crossing Hampstead Heath between the Spaniard's Inn and the footpath to Temple Fortune. A third occupied tea-time. The necessary fourth took a year of labor and passed through thirteen versions. Since Housman will not say which stanza is which, the critic is left with the task of reconstruction by hypothesis. Here is mine:

The first two stanzas were composed at a single stroke. They were necessarily the first, since the other two assume their thought and act as corollaries. (Though the thought of the fourth parallels that of the second, the first and fourth together do not make an understandable finished thought.) Tea-time produced the fourth stanza and a complete poem. But the whole three-stanza poem now lacked symmetry. It was a monster with two great tails. Housman's sense of strict form demanded an interjected stanza between the two conclusions, in order to give balance to the repetition and return, and to set the personal emotion in a more nearly universal framework. The last stanza written, therefore, was the third. Since its conception was more mechanical, logical, and willed, it took more time and pain, not rising so naturally from the Castalian spring. In spite of one perfect line, it still seems slightly extraneous—argument rather than poetry, an artificial limb designed to make a body acceptable to society.

I should now like to advance two points: (1) If someone else, more ingenious, proposed an explanation totally at variance with mine, no sufficient evidence exists to prove either of us right or wrong. (2) Yet if the genesis of this poem were known in exact detail, it would not only enable us to interpret this particular work with more precision, but in its revelation of the *method, order,* and *emphases* in Housman's mind as he worked at poetry, it would help us to understand more fully other poems by him, in their last nuances and most delicate discriminations.

Let us set against Housman's poem, in some detail, one which exists in various versions in the Lockwood Library— the "Missa Vocis" by Richard P. Blackmur. The two provide a neat comparison, not only because they fall into formal four-part balanced structures, but also because their common subject is the use and permanence of poetry. Blackmur's is harder to grasp. What light, let us ask, does the composition of a poem throw upon its meaning and its beauty? What difficulties in a finished poem may be explained, what pointless ambiguities dispelled, what purposeful ambiguities sharpened, by references found in its earlier states? Naturally, no one should claim that the study of all versions will necessarily make any and every poem crystal-clear. Words do not behave in such fashion, even when poets use them.

Here, then, as it appears in its published version in Blackmur's volume, *The Second World,* is:

MISSA VOCIS

Priest-mannerly the mind,
that president mask,
gives dogsight to the new blind,
priest-mannerly unknowing
what mastering ear-task
keeps the great churn going.

O unmannerable heart,
monk-dancer, be still,
be leashless, apart:
the sounding, the growing
unabettable will
sets the great churn going.

Lie chidden, lie dark,
in the reserved deep
lie prone, lie stark:
the unprayable flowing,
the vast sluiceage of sleep,
sets the great churn going.

In the wringing of new sound,
chance flowering to choice,
old words in full round
in-breathing, thrall-throwing;
the mass of new voice
keeps the great churn going.

A reader is struck first of all, I suppose, by unusual words that seem to contain much meat—such words as "priest-mannerly," "dogsight," "unmannerable," or "sluiceage." Yet in trying to tie their meanings into the poem precisely, he is soon struck also by the notable repetitions and contrasts that organize the poem and give definition to many of its words. Take "priest-mannerly." The first line defines "mind" in the form of a simple equation. If the mind is a priest, it is also a mask, a mask with the modifying adjective or noun-adjective "president." It is further associated with the blind, to whom it cannot give the best kind of sight (though dog-lovers may not agree). The mind, moreover, does not know true mastery. To aid in its definition in this poem, the priest-mind is set in opposition to the monk-dancer, the heart, with the further contrast of "mannerly" with "unmannerable." The religious imagery of the first two stanzas colors the last two, so that prayers (or rather, their absence) occur in the third stanza; while "the *mass* of new voice" is given its primary meaning of the sacrament (which might not otherwise be apparent, since it is not the most frequent meaning of the word), not only through the title but through the imagery that permeates and organizes the poem.

Similarly, the poem-in-itself may be used to explain, or give further and better meanings to, other words which it contains. That puzzling "dogsight," which at first I took to be connected with a dog's sense of smell, is made clearer by the word "leashless" in the corresponding point of the next stanza. Now the reader may conjure up a Seeing Eye dog—or, if he cares about consistency in imagery, perhaps a blind beggar with his dog before some cathedral. The "ear-task" ("Doth God exact day labor, light denied?") fills with more meaning as one comes to the sound, the words, the mass, the voice, the ringing, of the final stanza.

Indeed, the poem as it stands is so closely woven that one

feels confident that not one of its effects is an accident. Even
the simple words do not seem single in meaning. "Round" in
the last stanza is not only the full perfection of a circle but a
round of singing. It is more than coincidence that the "sound"
of the fourth stanza has its harbinger in the "sounding" of
the second stanza. And though the "wringing" of new sound
may mean primarily the strenuous process in harmonizing
the "Sphere-born harmonious sisters, Voice and Verse," it
may also suggest a joyous ringing chime of bells. (Housman,
by the way, uses this pun of wring-ring even more demon-
strably.) Are we now becoming too impossibly refined if we
point out that the negative "un-"s of the first three stanzas
change to "in-" in the final section, not in the sense of negation but of self-sufficiency? Mr. Blackmur, in his desire to
express the ineluctable, unabettable, unknowable infinite, has
used in other poems these mysterious negatives in "un-" and
"in-" until they have become almost a trademark for his writing. It is hardly without significance that they drop out in
the final positive section. Note, too, the single word that
changes in the powerful refrain. Almost purely by formal
means—by the balance throughout between sight and sound,
between negatives and positives, between the changed re-
frains—a logical structure could be set up for the poem: a
negative statement, or rebuttal, or unsatisfactory hypothesis,
is established in the first stanza; the next two stanzas fix a
groundwork and speculate concerning origins; the final stanza
states positively that art, not intellect—and art based on emotion and instinct—preserves, shall we say, the life of the spirit.
In view of the extreme conscious symmetry of the poem, evident even in the controlled alliteration, one might dare to
speculate that the adjective "what *mas*tering ear-task" sets
going at the start a query which is answered by an echoing
assertion in the same foot of the stanza in the last section: "the
mass of new voice."

But this is exactly the type of criticism which many people impatiently dismiss as finical and overnice. The critic, they maintain, is outdoing Arachne, spinning cobwebs out of himself which the poem itself cannot possibly support. Well, let us see. Let us turn to Mr. Blackmur's own actual earlier versions. We have so far applied the pure-esthetic technique of asking the poem to explain itself within its own self-contained limits. Let us now apply historical criticism—but historical criticism which few could consider irrelevant, since it will use solely the materials which the poet himself used in bringing his finished work into shape. And here, in six successive versions, one may watch in fascination as chance flowers into choice.

That fine alliterative opposition of chance and choice, so frequent in the poetry of William Butler Yeats, seems only one of the deliberate compliments which Blackmur pays to the Irish poet. One might profitably compare the structure of "Missa Vocis" with that of Yeats's four-stanzaed "Sailing to Byzantium." Moreover, the use of a vigorous refrain in homely language is reminiscent of Yeats's later poems. I shall have occasion later to mention again how sympathy with another poet, no less than the desire to describe faithfully the subject at hand, may mold a poem. Here one wonders if the faintly medieval ecclesiastic imagery may not be one of Yeats's many responsibilities. And as for "monk-dancer"— neglecting the old *sursum corda* idea of "My heart leaps up" —may it not have been dictated in part by Yeats's repeated symbol of the dancer? The "monk" half of it obviously ties in with the priest and the mass in imagery; I wish my own unmannerable heart did not also call up, because of "dog-sight" and "leashless," the idea of a monkey dancing on a string. The other versions do not help to make "monk-dancer" clearer, except the very first, where we have, instead, the much more flat "old traveler."

The sixth and final version gives the poem as it was published. The fifth version makes some definite commitments on parts which earlier had troubled Mr. Blackmur. There is an erasure of "hindsight" in place of "dogsight"—the only version in which that word is questioned—but since it is an erasure, perhaps we had better not play with it, except to use it as ghostly support for our earlier suspicion that dogsight is not a good thing. But in this fifth version, to finish up with canine matters, Blackmur settles on the certain and balanced:

> Lie chidden, lie dark.

This had begun as "Lie doggo be dark," and had persisted doggedly through later versions until the artist's sense that the whole is greater than the part led Blackmur to abandon a bad pun and rescue harmony in diction. Nevertheless, that almost catastrophic persistence of "doggo" through so many trials may help in understanding the vast sluiceage of sleep in the reserved deep—two lines that hold steady throughout.

A similar well-balanced line—"in-breathing, thrall-throwing"—comes to rest in the fifth version. The fourth had wavered between "in-breathed" and "in-breathing," each of which was an alternative for "breathed deep" in the second and third versions. This line took much work. That it was well worth the effort is obvious from its original form—"breathless tiptoeing"—which is so innocuous as almost to be deadly. The "breathless" is crossed out in favor of "flowering," and we can learn something of the working of a poet's mind from the way in which that fine word "flowering" was not discarded, even though it proved useless where first introduced, but was inserted instead in the line which read originally "Chance *deepening* to choice."

Version four considers altering the earlier "lie plumb" to "lie prone." Here again, the earlier and ultimately abandoned word "plumb" helps in the interpreting of the reserved deep and the vast sluiceage of sleep. This version also first invents the line "In the wringing of new sound." If it had seemed unwarranted at first reading to detect as overtone here the ringing of church bells, our speculation is now given more confidence when we see the original of this line:

The whole church of new sound.

Versions two and three merely play with punctuation, spelling, and compounds, and incorporate second-thoughts that are already suggested in the margin of the first (and only manuscript) version, which is easily the most interesting, and in which the poem, even at such an early stage, encounters forks in the trail and always takes the path toward sharper, fresher imagery and toward unity. Thus, the very first word of the first line—"Most mannerly the mind"—has "Priest" as an emendation in the margin, which increases the consistency and vividness of the imagery, and at the same time trades too much *rum-ram-ruf* on the letter "m" for a more powerful binding alliteration between "priest" and "president" in the next line.

Most revealing are some jottings that float free at the right-hand top of the page. Are these not the true germs of the poem?

only the voice
keeps the great churn going
sluicage of sleep
only the flowing

One cluster of marginal words that has nothing to do with the poem will make any of us who scribble verses self-conscious: "none" "atone" "moan" "drone" "tone" "stone" "alone." This is journeyman stuff, fit matter for the rhyming dictionary; it is mentioned here merely because it does call our attention to the rhyme words or sounds which Blackmur actually decided upon, to his care in choosing solid monosyllables, to their fine contrasts in adjacent lines, and their equally fine correspondences over larger areas, so that in rhyme as well as in thought stanzas one and four are allied, as are two and three. And never (except possibly in "thrall-throwing"?) does the poet's thought seem enslaved to his powerful, exact, and rewarding rhyme.

If any doubt remains that such painstaking revisions are worth the candle, I suggest that you compare the finished version with this earliest form:

> Most mannerly the mind,
> that president mask,
> makes dogsight the new blind.
> Most mannerly unknowing
> what mastering task
> keeps the great churn going
>
> O unmannerable heart,
> old traveler, be still,
> be leashless, apart:
> the sounding, the growing
> unabettable will
> sets the great churn going
>
> Lie doggo be dark
> in the reserved deep
> lie plumb, lie stark:
> the unprayable flowing
> the vast sluicage of sleep
> sets the great churn going
>
> The whole church of new sound
> chance deepening to choice
> old words in full round
> breathless tiptoeing:
> the mass of new voice
> keeps the great churn going

What is the sum of all these minute considerations? First, that a work of art may have extremely small beginnings—in this instance merely the persistent refrain of the great churn, plus a few tied-in images of sound and of liquidity which the churn itself might suggest. Second, at least to judge from Blackmur's rougher notes, that a poem may develop by giving a kind of metaphysical skeleton to its initial inspiration— working it out, perhaps, as mental propositions in a triple or quadruple division (here, finally: mind, heart/will, the unconscious, voice). Third, that a poem may be sketched as a whole, including weak padded lines that must later be changed, but also including phrases that are already finished and characteristic—in Blackmur's case the startling adjectives and nouns, the "great churn" itself, the "sluiceage of sleep," "mannerly," "dogsight," "leashless," as well as the magisterial and ominously abstract "unknowing," "unmannerable," "unabettable," and "unprayable." Fourth—and this comes with the sense of discovery—that at some point in composition a spark may flash that will illuminate the whole; a sudden insight may develop into a nervous system that brings the whole body alive. In this poem the spark sprang from the religious imagery. It is not present in the seed-kernel, "only the voice keeps the great churn going." In the original draft the *liquid* imagery which the churn may have initiated is developed only in the third stanza, and is expanded in no later versions. The *sound* imagery, dominated by the voice, never expands through the entire poem. And in the sketch as first set down there is no religious imagery until "unprayable" late in the third stanza. But at some moment, somehow, something clicks and it all becomes clear. Before the draft is put aside, we have in the last stanza "The whole *church* of new sound"; "only the voice" has become "the *mass* of new voice" at the end; the same title in Latin, "*Missa Vocis,*" has been added at the beginning; and in the margins as afterthoughts appear the mannerly *priest* and the dancer *monk*. Now the poem is so ecclesiastically colored throughout that Blackmur can change the first line of the last stanza to "In the wringing of new sound" and still leave the whole church in it by implication.

And finally among these conclusions: that the progress of an artist in creation is always toward greater purity, intensity, and unity—in short, toward greater significance. The changes are small, but their cumulative effect should furnish an impressive lesson that the control and the form that make daydreams into art are not the results of happy accidents but of happy contrivings. Chance flowers into choice only when it is carefully tended.

I realize that such criticism as we have just gone through in the preceding paragraphs demands concentrated attention. I believe that such literary genetics can be carried on with profit only in detailed analyses. And later I should like to consider, in almost as leisurely a fashion, several other poems as further samples of the ore that waits to be mined. But we might here take a breather, change the intensive for the extensive view, and look at the wide variety of exciting trails that lead out from Buffalo. I cannot be fair in short space to any individual poet; I am even less fair, in this haphazard rambling, to those left out. And, though it should go without saying, the interest of a poem to a geneticist in literary criticism need be in no direct ratio to its worth.

The manuscripts themselves, as mere physical objects, often tell us something. Poetry suddenly becomes a part of life in a sharp, usually unsuspected way, when we see in the case of one of the few writers of verse who makes his calling pay handsomely, that his copyright is typed as part of the original worksheet.

Or when we look at William Carlos Williams' first drafts

written sprawled crossways on his prescription blanks at Rutherford, New Jersey.

Or when we find that Margaret Fishback has rescued crumpled scraps of light verse from the wastebasket, scraps in which we can trace how the *mot passable* becomes the *mot juste* or the *bon mot* even when it is transformed, as she tells us, in spite of such handicaps as sitting under a hair-drier or walking along the street. And in passing we may wonder whether epigrammatic verse is the natural poetry of the modern cities partly because there is time to compose only in scraps.

Or when we discover the manuscript of a grim and atypical poem by Ogden Nash on man's unescapable loneliness, developed in Wordsworthian ballad stanzas, serving also as a worksheet on which bud those rhymes typical of Nash's inventive genius and doubtless used by him elsewhere: "countenance—mountains," "acquaintance—maintenance," "enthusiasm—as choosy as 'm."

These minor amusements are surface manifestations showing that some interest may reside in the sheer material state of the manuscripts themselves. But if we dig a little deeper, we find that the worksheets reveal the character of the composer, or authenticate traits that we have uncertainly sensed in their published works.

We need not be graphologists to see that Wallace Stevens is fastidious, patterned, singing, sure. The arrangement and minor changes of his drafts tell us so.

Marianne Moore's corrections, though few, are wholly convincing as to her delicate watchworks. In each artifact, hers is a precision rhyme-piece. Every comma looms a comet; every syllable must tick in place.

Although it would take months to assimilate fully the gargantuan collections for Dylan Thomas's long poem "The

Ballad of the Long-Legged Bait," five minutes is enough to confirm the impression of his unmatched and unreined imagination, the prodigality and massiveness of his sensual symbolism which would make a whole school of fleshly poets look like minnows.

Robert Frost in any individual poem seems to write all of a piece. Does the poem mature in meditation, compose itself mentally, that he is able to set down as a first draft a completed copy that requires only four changes? The Library has the original version, written on notebook paper, of his fine poem "The Silken Tent"—so unified and convincing a blend of thought, imagery, and wording that one is able to do no more than say, It is there. Three of the changes are minor. One takes a bumpiness out of the meter; one corrects a flatness; a third replaces a simple image with another more spacious and free. The only important change is to cross out the original title, "In Praise of Your Poise," in favor of "The Silken Tent." Such a drive toward impersonality and concreteness, away from sentiment and autobiography, is indeed one of the most significant and well-attested processes in poetic composition that the collection as a whole demonstrates.

Walter de la Mare also, no less than Frost, works as an expert craftsman. In his early draft of "The Empty House" his revisions are made principally for the sake of meter, for which he probably possesses the most sensitive of living ears. In the delicate shifting of the "Il Penseroso" tetrameter, which veers from trochaic to iambic, he works over any line in which the metrical reading would be puzzling or doubtful at first trial. For instance, since the line

> Moss too is mouldering slow

is not ample enough to carry on the meter even as a variant, he corrects it to

> Lichen too is mouldering slow.

And then—since "too" always looks suspiciously like metrical padding, and since in the actual poem it has no logical referent—he prints it finally as:

> Every stone is mouldering slow.

But in addition to the confirmations which the collection supplies with regard to the preoccupations, the ruling passions, the dominant instincts of individual poets, the Library is rich in examples which illustrate more general principles of composition by which a poem comes right.

I would mention Robert Hillyer's various versions of "A Letter to Queen Nefertiti," which appears in his volume *A Letter to Robert Frost*. Taken together, they add up to a classic and complete example of gradual crystallization and selection of the final images and words.

Or consider as an occasional poem, a *poème voulu*, the half-dozen versions of Malcolm Cowley's "Tomorrow Morning." Though it never becomes thoroughly convincing, it shows the continuous struggle to strip off rhetoric and second-hand experience. In its first versions, while one respects the emotion that generates the lines, one is made uneasy by the attitudes and symbols that are clichés, by a kind of falseness which actually seems born of the style itself. Its Spanish People's Army appears a little too posed and strained. Yet Cowley works steadily toward economy and clips the extravagances. Thus, in the early notes is the picture: "On the steps of the Cathedral is a dead comrade, his arms hacked off, his blood flowing in two streams toward the gutter." After many trials this eventuates as:

> A corpse was sprawled on the cathedral steps;
> ours, for I knew his features in the beam
> of a pocket flashlight.

Or again, such a hollowness as:

> but our lives were good to live and our deaths to die

turns a little away from Fourth-of-July speeches toward Hemingway in:

> and yet our lives were good, the blood in our mouths had the good taste of tomorrow.

and finally irons out into:

> Think back on us, the martyrs and the traitors,
> the cowards even, swept by the same flood
> of passion toward the morning that is yours:
> O children born from, nourished with our blood.

Cowley's poem, then, conceived in somewhat extravagant passion and carried at length toward a certain dignity and simplicity and sincerity, shows the road of the poet.

There is a typescript opening for Elinor Wylie's long poem "Miranda's Supper," which is a kind of inverted "My Last Duchess" laid in Virginia in 1866. It has Miss Wylie's own corrections in pencil. I would like to mention one correction, because it shows clearly a problem which confronts many poets—the adjustment of some important symbol, some "objective correlative" for an emotion, until it seems satisfactory. Miss Wylie's search here is to get a figure that will be mentioned only briefly, yet that must stand for the hateful Northern intruders in an exhausted South, and that also must key in with the aristocratic tone of the whole poem. Miss Wylie gives up Yale for Harvard. The original setting runs:

> She never made her anger oral.
> An ivory face, expertly graven,
> Met the Colonel from New Haven.
> She used him like a prince's legate,
> But, O, her eyes, her eyes were agate!

And then, crossing out the wrong pair of lines—poets can be so careless when they revise for their own eyes!—she pencils in the margin:

> She remained a marble memory
> To the Cambridge Captain Amory;

The most important criticism of art, as T. S. Eliot has maintained, is the criticism made by the artist himself during the process of creation—inventing, selecting, rejecting, harmonizing, contrasting, unifying, articulating, ordering, clarifying, repeating, rounding, polishing, sharpening, emphasizing, arranging, finishing. In a word: deciding. His decree is absolute, though it is subject to his own later one-man referendum. Furthermore, the artist ought to be his own best critic, since no one else can ever know his subject more intimately or view his work with such complete sympathy. One more reason, then, why the study of poets' worksheets should afford the closest approximation to pure criticism which is available to those of us who are not the poets themselves.

Hildegarde Flanner has left the clearest examples in the collection of the poet acting as his own critic and teacher. Up and down her margins she strings her checks and crosses, her queries and affirmations that chant their critic chorus. Again, she will offer herself a generous display of words, listing synonyms in profusion; then choosing. An early typewritten version of "O motor, motors" is aureoled with alternatives. In this poem the improvements can be traced through the three versions and cannot be mistaken. What began in a style almost as lax as a commencement ode, ends as a metaphysical success.

The most exhaustive revisings which I looked at were carried out by Will Gibson in his twenty-line poem "Timberline." There are eighty—count them: eighty—numbered versions. In each version Mr. Gibson's sharply individualized technique explores a few lines, making lavish variations. Then, line by line, he selects, consolidates, stamps approval, and marches on to the next battle and choice. It is exciting to watch the final discovery of

> the witchland of freak growth, dwarf hags of wood

from such a tangle of trials and hazards as "margin," "badlands," "highlands," "torture," "twists"; then *witchland*. Or "dwarf tree, hag tree," "dwarf and hag in tree," "dwarf bole, hag limb," "dwarf twists of wood"; then the compressed animistic *dwarf hags of wood*. Here, too, the stuff that makes poetry is revealed in the unending struggle between subject and technique, between timberline in the Rockies and Gerard Manley Hopkins, for Mr. Gibson knows them both intimately. It would be hard to say whether "rock peace" owes more to Hopkins or to the feeling one gets at times in that high clear air on the mountain slopes where the trees give up their drawn ghosts. "Rock peace" is sired, in these multiversions, by "rock slide" out of "rock piece." And for the final version of

> rock peace, rock peace, to grow
> red thrifts of lichen rust,

I should like to list some of the variants on this trail toward Hopkinsian compression and toward simultaneous suggestions of emotion, life and death, struggle and peace, the hard cold penury of the timberline, all realized in colorful concreteness:

> Here is a rock peace in snow
> . . . for crows / and conies to nest.

> Here is a rock peace that grows dead lichens.

> . . . to grow lichens and starvers

> lichens no deeper than tints.

thrifts of lichen on flint. [What part do rhyme and assonance play here in the progress to new versions?]

red thrifts of lichen and flint.

red thrifts of lichen, merely.

rust thrifts of lichen, dead.

And then: *red thrifts of lichen rust.*

Sir Edward Marsh's manuscript volumes of La Fontaine's fables offer generous answers to the special poser of translation. They show the triple pull toward literal accuracy in translating, or toward fidelity to La Fontaine's colloquial, racy, chatty, informal style, piquantly preserved at times by a dash of archaic diction, or toward determination to create something in English that will stand as a poem in its own right. I quote below three openings for "A Saying of Socrates." They indicate that a translator may be faithful without being a slave. The reader may decide which he would publish, and if he wishes help from La Fontaine, he may turn to IV, 17, of the *Fables:*

> One day the builders had in hand
> A house for Socrates the wise.
> A group stood round to criticize
> The way the edifice was planned.
> The first remarks, "I must aver
> That the interior seems to me
> Unworthy of your character."
> Another blames the front, and all agree
> The rooms are of a miserable size—

> A house was built for Socrates, the Wise,
> Which everyone combined to criticize.
> One thought th' internal decoration
> Unworthy of his reputation:

> Another blamed the front, and all
> Agreed the rooms were far too small—
>
> A house was built for Socrates,
> Which generally failed to please.
> One thought th' interior decoration . . . etc.

And which do you prefer among:

> Old Socrates was right in this!
>
> The true Socratic wisdom this!

and

> The right Socratic wisdom this!

William Carlos Williams has given a number of versions of his poems which show his care with words, spacing, and revaluing. He, as well as Laura Riding, have contributed manuscript lectures on poetry. Anyone who accepts Williams' ideas of the importance of objective form—"A poem is an object . . . in which words are associated with the form to produce a meaning"—will note with interest the changes he himself makes, not only in line lengths but in stanzaic divisions, and will gauge what may be the change in total meaning which such formal variants bring about.

This has been a brief tour, something like a sprint through the Metropolitan Museum of Art in fifteen minutes. We have glimpsed such variety as Margaret Fishback's light verse, William Carlos Williams' little poems on prescription blanks, Ogden Nash working at cock-eyed rhymes, Wallace Stevens' elegance, Marianne Moore's delicacy, Dylan Thomas's ebullience, Robert Frost's economical certainty, Walter de la Mare's flawless metrical taste, Robert Hillyer's crystallization, Malcolm Cowley's working toward the disciplining of emotion, Elinor Wylie's choosing of a symbol, Hildegarde

Flanner's expressed self-criticism, Will Gibson's fighting it out on this line and the next if it takes all summer, Sir Edward Marsh's felicities as a translator. And these brief glances have been grouped roughly around such larger issues as the physical impact of the worksheets themselves, the usefulness of these poems-in-generation in turning opinion into knowledge concerning a poet's deepest roots, and the artist's perpetual problems of controlling, choosing, communicating, improving, and of relating himself to society, or his technique to his subject, or his intense emotional vagaries to the cold, clear, impersonal demands of form.

After such diversity, which has been far too sketchily presented, but which may have served to show both the range of the collection and possible applications of the genetic approach, we may turn back to a fuller analysis of one piece of work by each of five poets: Robert Bridges, Genevieve Taggard, Louis MacNeice, Conrad Aiken, and Stephen Spender. In intention these little studies will comprise five candid and unposed portraits of artists at work.

Robert Bridges' almost medieval handwriting would indicate to the most innocent amateur the positiveness of his thought. In the three manuscript pages of *The Testament of Beauty* which the Lockwood Memorial Library possesses—two original worksheets, plus a copy of the first page of the manuscript poem—the minute and frequent and meticulous changes show him working toward precision in pictorial illustration or in emotional keying of his thought or toward grammatical clarity, arguing with himself about referents for pronouns, excising an unnecessary inversion, supplying more specific nouns in place of general phrases or toward a more beautiful flow in the rhythm of his loose Alexandrines, so that his ear has cunningly tested and weighed each phrase, line, and verse-paragraph until its premeditated art carries to the reader the joy of unpremeditated grace. In these pages he tests out in light pencilstrokes the feet of each measure; here the light tentative pencilmarks finally become the bold red ink of correction; and through it all the certainty of his central thought and rhythm, played over glancingly by an arabesque of metrical variation and a continual balancing of alternatives in illustration, phrasing, grammar, articulation, convey so sharply to the looker-on a sense of watching an artist at work as almost to belie the skeptical statement with which Bridges closes page 46 of his manuscript:

> How in itself
> Reason is powerless showeth when philosophers
> will treat of ART, the which they are apt to do
> having good intuition that their master key
> that they most need may lie therein: *

Perhaps the reason of the philosophers is powerless; but in spite of Robert Bridges' Olympian reproach, as we look closely at the revisions of his manuscript, we feel that observation, more humble than reason, here comes close to the growth of a poet's mind, and learns, perhaps, some of the secrets of his art.

Where does the life of a poem reside? Perhaps this question belongs with the ancient and unanswerable, Where is the

---

* That the Lockwood Library manuscript is an early though important version, and that Bridges continued his minute improvements in expression while holding firm to his central thought, may be brought out by comparing this version with the lines as they appear in the 1929 Oxford University Press edition of *The Testament of Beauty*, New York, pp. 70-71, Book II, lines 751-755:

> How in its naked self
> Reason wer powerless showeth when philosophers
> wil treat of Art, the which they are full ready to do,
> having good intuition that their master-key
> may lie therein: but since they must lack vision of Art . . .

seat of the soul? Yet each of us has felt, for some poem, This phrase is its center, this stanza is the heart, this bit is worth all the rest. In considering Blackmur's "Missa Vocis," we made our way back from speculations on the finished product toward the groundwork of its inception. Let us try the experiment in reverse, taking as our subject Genevieve Taggard's "The Four Songs." In the end, this poem settled to stability, so that the final version in the 1938 *Collected Poems* varies from its 1934 publications in *Poetry* and in Miss Taggard's *Not Mine to Finish* volume only in a few punctuation changes, one section-division omitted, and one plural changed to a singular. The poem is finished, confident, wide in implication and deep in thought, universal in its subject. Yet it began in uncertainties. Let us look at its first stirrings in Capri, 1931, and Mallorca, 1932. The fifteen pages of its worksheets are written on all kinds of paper and at all times, and though we must separate some of its tangled threads, which comes first cannot always be ascertained, and of course many exist simultaneously.

Consider the title, to begin with, which to some poets (like Marianne Moore) is integral to the poem, and which to others is a mere afterthought, or no more than a number—Opus 110, say. As a title "The Four Songs" is cool and unrevealing. Yet in the typescript at the end of the worksheets, dated "Bennington College," it is entitled "Poet to Lover (Admitting Limitation)." This title, and particularly the parenthesis, should prove of value in interpreting the complete poem, even though in the interests of impersonality it was eventually abandoned. But there are other discarded titles. There is "Poet to Plain-Reader"; there is "Poet to Ordinary Man," though the "ordinary" is circled and questioned; there is an intrusive and undeveloped title of "Asphodel," that flower that strews the gray plains of Hades and is related, poetically as well as etymologically, to the daffodil-narcissus. In short, the titles suggest that this will be a song, to a lover, or plain-reader, or ordinary man, whose nature cannot be satisfactorily fixed. The trail is lost.

Let us make another start from the subtitle "Admitting Limitations." What are the limitations? One short scrap begins

> Oh person who must bear the weight
> Of ideal lover,

peters out in a questionmark and a jiggle, and ends "Poor person!" Yet there are many quick sketches of that poor person, each of which gets no further than a line or two before it is discarded:

> Songs to deaf ears are often and often sung.

[For some time, this line seemed to be the true start of the poem.]

> The impervious ear of a statue of beaten bronze

> You will not hear . . .

> reader, impervious, in the pride
> of one who . . .

> Plain reader, you will be the ear

But the reader will not be a very good ear; an adjective is needed—a two-syllable adjective, the worksheet tells us—and thinking back perhaps unconsciously to the earlier statue of beaten bronze, Miss Taggard inserts "sculptured."

The limitations, then, lie to some extent in the subject addressed. Here is no conjunction, but an opposition, of minds; and fate so enviously debars them through temperamental disparities. Proud, deaf, impervious, the plain-reader is too ordinary (though that is questioned), too plain, or perhaps is capable of reading only what is plainly expressed.

How else should it be expressed, except plainly? Or how else can it? Part of the limitations comes from the inadequacy of language in the face of fact. Silence almost seems better, or truer:

> I will revoke all singing words to hear
> What hangs between two people.

And:

> I will have silence follow while I wait
> For that unworded part I wish in you.

Yet a poet knows that "I court with sound," since it is his instrument, his gift. Nevertheless, the dissatisfaction with words continues:

> No poet may no matter how gold his tongue
> Choose any word . . .

And almost in disgust: "our fancy language"!

Limitations exist in the poet as well. Little phrases that are never again used show the unrest and the blank wall:

> the blunted sorrow in a winter's storm

> For us, since here we deviate
> Become ourselves, a helpless me and you—

> So, if I would, I could not help you [though this is
> emended to "could not *much* help you"].

Or perversely, another blind alley:

> I will grow silent, separate [or: stubborn] selfishly
> Spying on all I cannot see in you.

Or in humorous despair, quite out of key:

> I took a crack in a hotel ceiling
> In preference to thoght and feeling.

Poor reader! Poor language! Poor poet! Housman's speculation seems borne out: that art grows out of irritation, like a pearl secreted from the painful particle of sand in the oyster's shell. Yet the world must be shattered into bits, and then remolded nearer to the heart's desire. Language *must* be made to serve. And still, still— One is reminded of Vaughan's lines:

> But to write true, unfeignéd verse
> Is very hard.

Miss Taggard is aware of the painful difficulty, and will write—it grows into a finer paradox in the finished poem—

> with frank [or: candid] recitent [for: reticent] art.

But how to proceed? Through what means that are available to the poet? Not through immediate realism. There are no hotel ceilings in the finished poem. And she will not develop the early sketch, half crossed out:

> Plain-reader, over-coated, gone from view
> Across the city block . . .

Perhaps Eliot's speculation is also borne out: that the progress of an artist is not toward the expression of personality, but toward the extinction of, the escape from, personality.

Yet somehow, as in all poetry, things that are seen and heard must be made to convey the unseen. Images and symbols are the stuff of poetry. Paradoxically, again, objects must be made to express what they do not express. Impossibilities must be murdered. In a powerful quintuple rush of negatives she fronts the problem:

> Nothing you see in Nature, no, nothing,
> Part of myself no bare outline
> Could plot for you, nor ever I sing . . .

Nothing in Nature, no, nothing. And yet inevitably she turns to what she has more than thrice denied. An early abandoned title which I have not mentioned is "Poet as Farmer." Not until about midway in the rough drafts does this thread become notable, as Miss Taggard proceeds to farm Nature. Here again, there is the ceaseless struggle between negation and affirmation, between what words cannot do for the plain reader and what they do do for the poet:

> No pantomime of moon . . .

Or later:

> We need no pantomime
> Of moon or jocund sun.

But also:

> . . . pantomime of moon or sun
> Take them as gifts.

Again comes a phrase:

> Then since no symbol hangs upon the sea . . .

Yet this too loses its negation:

> Only a metaphor of natural things.

The drive is toward the positive, toward creation. It is worth noting that eventually this poem was published in *Poetry*, with two other pieces, under the general title of "Affirmations." The resolution of the creating poet, in the midst of paradox, comes out powerfully in the lines:

> Something I will make clear in my own time
> Without the aid of metaphors and moons.

The affirmative note is becoming clearer. The bewildered and unsatisfying uncertainties are giving way before more universal and assured statements:

> Use these four songs to know the *general* heart.

Language itself is becoming tractable, more fitted and molded to imperious and continuing demands:

> I give to you, elaborated [no! re-worked; no! re-worded], with all my heart.

Suddenly, the crystallization. The mosaic bits, the shards and orts, the velleities, come together in a flash, and for the first time, organized and confident, a manuscript page starts the poem with its rightful beginning:

> Four songs I'll sing to you
> From the four seasons taken.

The third line slips into:

> All of them fond and true,

but this is quickly corrected to a "truer," more comprehensive and impersonal reading:

> Each of them partly true.

We have reached the crest, and the rest of the way is downhill.

This analysis of beginnings has been lengthy and detailed because so very few such analyses can be found anywhere. Yet there is plentiful evidence in the Buffalo Collection that many poems come into being through a comparable process: slowly, or painfully, or after false starts, so that at first there is no way of knowing which are the trails that lead nowhere and which are the vital motifs that will expand and become clear. Poetry, too, has its Venus Genetrix. Although the goddess is veiled, and although a complete anatomy even were it possible would be blasphemous, a serious attempt to trace her lineaments, to look toward what may stand revealed, cannot be irreverent. We feel that we are watching a drama whose end deliberately unfolds. The process is one of translation: uncertainty becomes certainty, the vague becomes clear, irritation and unrest become irony and gaiety. Generalized art at last works its way free from personal sentiment, like a butterfly breaking from an outworn cocoon.

As the climax and reward of such long choosing, it is time to set down the finished poem in all its cool limpidity:

THE FOUR SONGS

Four songs I'll sing to you
From the four seasons taken,
Each of them partly true; . . .
Showing you how once-shaken
Like autumn; like winter, stoic, sad;
Elated like early spring
I am; like summer, equally laden
With fruit of matron-mind and maiden.
Four songs I'll sing
To you,—flute voices anyone
Might, from all nature fancy and seize on;
Since it is well in singing songs to you
I should select those clear and general
Moods-in-the-earth mankind has known so well,
Four songs I'll sing to you,
And amply sing.

But to these affirmations will you add
—Nothing you see in nature, no, nothing—

Something no summer mirrors, an outline
No moon will stamp with her official shine,
Something not sung by me, but mine;
Added, if added, by its like in you.

Four songs I'll sing to you.
False, candid art!
So much of me as is not me
I give to you, re-worded, with all my heart.
Then, done with seasons, sun and moon and sea,
Knowing their symbols no more than little-true,
I wait the sure rejoinder,—monody
That comes when I am done, from listening you.
What else I am you are implored to sense
At your own pains. Our odd identity
Cannot be sung. In us, this difference
No metaphor from nature can supply.
So if I would, I could not further, I,
Whose words past this monotony are all mistaken;
Four songs I'll sing to you, never to die
From the four seasons taken.

For fear that the untenable argument may develop, that
every poem must be begotten by despair upon impossibility,
let us immediately set down for comment an impressionistic
poem by Louis MacNeice that seems to have come easily. In
his *Poems 1925-40* it is entitled "Entirely":

If we could get the hang of it entirely
    It would take too long;
All we know is the splash of words in passing
    And falling twigs of song,
And when we try to eavesdrop on the great
    Presences it is rarely
That by a stroke of luck we can appropriate
    Even a phrase entirely.

If we could find our happiness entirely
    In somebody else's arms
We should not fear the spears of the spring nor the city's
    Yammering fire alarms
But, as it is, the spears each year go through
    Our flesh and almost hourly
Bell or siren banishes the blue
    Eyes of Love entirely.

And if the world were black or white entirely
    And all the charts were plain
Instead of a mad weir of tigerish waters,
    A prism of delight and pain,
We might be surer where we wished to go
    Or again we might be merely
Bored but in brute reality there is no
    Road that is right entirely.

With this poem I played a little game, noting the words or phrases that seemed to me particularly fine discoveries before I turned to the worksheets to see if they had not cost much labor. The results are hardly conclusive. The "prism" and the "mad weir of tigerish waters" could not be checked, for that third stanza, with some of Mr. MacNeice's best wry philosophizing, was not to be found in the first draft. "Spears" in the second stanza was there from the beginning. On the other hand, "Yammering" is a later invention that makes the original "Screaming" sound weakly raucous. And for "Eyes of Love" he had originally written the lazier "Anyone else."

The elastic metrical substitutions, the false rhymes and the run-on lines and quick veerings of the thought, endow the poem with spontaneity. I must confess I had expected to find that this freshness and simplicity, as so often happens, came from travail. Not so this time. In three instances only does Mr. MacNeice work deftly to maintain his informal tone. He began by eavesdropping "on the *gods*," changed it to "on the *dark,*" and then decided upon "the *great.*" The blithe "by a stroke of luck we can appropriate" passed through the earlier dull and literal: "we can catch and then appropriate." Last of all, originally he had written that "the spears each year go through Our *hands.*" The more particular reference here would certainly have roused images inappropriate to the poem, and wisely "hands" is replaced by "flesh."

The penciled version of the first two stanzas, then, surprises us by the surety with which it seems jotted down in swift abbreviations, as if the poem were already singing in his head. In the same little blue spiral-ringed notebook that contains the germs of so many of his poems, the second version of "Entirely," neatly inked in between the address of the *Southern Review* and some doodling, appears as in its published state, including the sure phrases of the third stanza and the delicately precise, ironically casual, concluding four lines.

The poem, of course, may have started elsewhere. But the little blue book is actually a poet's closed garden. I wish we had more of them. A poet is not only a maker, but a finder— a trouvère or troubadour. Often he will lose his suddenly discovered nuggets if he does not collect them in some such sort of pouch as Mr. MacNeice's commonplace book—or rather, uncommonplace book. It contains a few witty discoveries, sketched phrases to be salted away, epigrams that suggest again how often complete poems are started, or written, in little spurts that leave the composer breathless after a couplet. (Parenthetically, I might mention that Mr. MacNeice's Iceland journal is also a treasure chest bound with irony, particularly the rather wicked notes for his Testament, which leaves to hundreds of people Dantesque legacies. They get what was coming to them.)

If word-for-word analysis did not make almost impossibly difficult reading, or if there were some way to print on this page various versions superposed, I would like to give here the three typewritten drafts of Conrad Aiken's "Sursum Corda," published as the first of his *Brownstone Eclogues*. As it is, I shall merely give the final version, with a few comments as to why its close study would show genetic criticism operating perhaps at its most characteristic:

> Speak to us only with the killer's tongue,
> the animal madness of the fierce and young:
> and from that agony we'll learn to break
> our human hearts, but for thy suffering's sake.
>
> Then will the mind, exploring passion, learn   5
> through all this burning world how thou dost burn:
> in every particle, and hour, thy death,
> in every painful leaf the creative breath.
>
> And thy stone's hardness, we will learn this too,
> with our wet flesh, our flesh as soft as dew;   10
> through this small looking-glass to guess at length
> the savage knowledges beyond our strength.
>
> Wherever death's red hand unhusks a heart,
> or tiger ice rips the meek hills apart,
> there we lie down alone, and lonely spend   15
> the spirit's silence to the spirit's end.
>
> Lost from thy rock-face to thy last abyss,
> we faint in darkness for an age; yet this
> ends in an hour; and in the sun with thee
> we wear the rainbow and the rain, and see: 20
> we break the numbers and the names, and see:
> we are thyself, thy heart of light, and see.

This poem appears tightly organized and powerfully controlled toward a single effect. Moreover, the organization seems intellectual, so that the poem leans less toward the pole of instinctive song than toward that of disciplined reflection. (The reader need only remember Dante and Milton to realize that I am here making a mere descriptive classification of method, not setting up any order of merit.) Looking at the world's brutality today, Mr. Aiken conceives a metaphysical drama of savageness and salvation, or of savageness leading to salvation, and clothes this bipartite conception in words and images that insistently intensify one part or the other of his dichotomy.

At some time every poem must have its vision; all the rest is revision. And Mr. Aiken's three typewritten versions, which are all different from the printed poem as given above, clearly typify what is the norm for the Lockwood Library worksheets of all its poets—the shaping of material toward a sharper clarity and unity through countless minute, loving alterations. The vision, the flash of insight—Benedetto Croce's intuition—has no history in time, though it may have a pre-history that can be studied on the page, as we have seen with Miss Taggard's poem. What *can* be studied in the creative process of poetry is the revision, as if the original idea were a statue being chipped loose from the rock by a multitude of deliberate little strokes. The manuscripts attest, somewhat less lugubriously, the truth of Arnold's lines:

> Tasks in hours of insight will'd
> Can be through hours of gloom fulfill'd.

Yet if this essay cannot collect all the chips of marble, it might at least suggest again that earlier versions may act as guides in interpreting individual passages in the finished poem. For instance, in line 5 I could not be sure that "passion" legitimately contained, as perhaps its primary meaning, the

limited sense of Christ's passion, his last sufferings and agony
on the cross, until I saw the line in its earlier form:

> Yes, of that agony the mind shall learn . . .

Similarly "creative breath" in line 8 is given additional mul-
tiplex precision by an earlier alternative, "new birth." The
Rock of Ages imagery is evident enough in the final section,
but one might be troubled as to whether "thy stone" in line
9 might also allude, with seeming irrelevance, to Christ's
calling of Peter. Again one is reassured by an earlier version:
"And the rocks hardness."

The intense "we faint in darkness for an age" has grown
out of the rather insipid "we drown, unknowing, for an age"
and "we sleep for an age in darkness." Even here, what is
finally written can be read more confidently after acquaintance
with the poem as a palimpsest. And the terrible contrasts between Christ and the tiger that give nerves to the poem are
intensified by one invention—the substitution of the word
"meek" for "red" in the earlier form of line 14:

> or tiger ice rips the red hills apart.

This whole stanza was not part of the earliest draft.

One most happy major change among so many small ones
assures us that even in the midst of deliberate labor, a poet
may hope that the best is yet to be. The last four lines really
make the poem and justify the title. Yet in the first version
they are a weak two:

> one moment comes, when, in the sun with thee,
> we shall be blind with pain and joy, but see.

The second version still tinkers with this couplet. Then comes
the reward, the discovery, with its fine triple chanting in
Paradiso imagery, which brings the poem to proportion and

a confident close. We cannot turn through the collection without realizing that inspiration is often the child of prolonged hard work.

And now let us take as a final coda and summary the genesis of Stephen Spender's famous piece, printed as Number xxiii in his 1933 *Poems:*

I think continually of those who were truly great.
Who, from the womb, remembered the soul's history
Through corridors of light where the hours are suns
Endless and singing. Whose lovely ambition
Was that their lips, still touched with fire,   5
Should tell of the Spirit clothed from head to foot in song.
And who hoarded from the Spring branches
The desires falling across their bodies like blossoms.

What is precious is never to forget
The essential delight of the blood drawn from ageless springs   10
Breaking through rocks in worlds before our earth.
Never to deny its pleasure in the morning simple light
Nor its grave evening demand for love.
Never to allow gradually the traffic to smother
With noise and fog the flowering of the spirit.   15

Near the snow near the sun, in the highest fields
See how these names are fêted by the waving grass
And by the streamers of white cloud
And whispers of wind in the listening sky.
The names of those who in their lives fought for life   20
Who wore at their hearts the fire's centre.
Born of the sun they travelled a short while towards the sun,
And left the vivid air signed with their honour.

Spender's large cloth-bound ledger which he calls "Sketch Book III," with a date on the outside of September, 1931, contains many of his best poems.* The poem above exists in five separate versions, each a stage in its shaping. I shall note only a few of the main crossroads, since a complete analysis would occupy this whole essay.

First of all, the evident passionately concentrated energy in revision should convince anyone that an unrhymed poem in irregular lines is not necessarily easy to write—or more important, that there is great difference between the free verse of a poet and the loose verse of a poetaster.

The honey of generation for this poem was a feeling of exaltation, inspired, it would seem, by some actual experience—high thought and emotion springing from contact with the Nature of Wordsworth, or of Senancour and Rousseau. The first line written, and crossed out, reads approximately:

I also have walked round the corner of that mountain at morning.

The second start on this first draft already contains in three lines the seeds of both the first and third sections of the completed poem:

> I think continually of those who were great
> I walk to the highest field and there near the snow
> But still under waving grass I read their names.

These lines also are crossed out. The original penciled version continues to mix the two themes of great men and a high, free landscape as it takes a fresh start:

Their names are hidden in the highest fields
Near the sun near the snow and under the waving grass.
Stand far above the villages and dots of men . . .

---

* The process of poetic creation as analyzed by the poet himself may profitably be studied in Stephen Spender's article, "The Making of a Poem," which appears on pages 294-308 in the summer issue, 1946, of the *Partisan*

But again, this last line is crossed out, and Mr. Spender never returns to a localized landscape, which he has already twice suggested only to reject. Though it may have begun with an occasion, therefore, this is not to be an occasional poem.

The fourth and final impulse on this first draft, while still beating back to the persistent central theme, now first considers why or how the great are great:

> I think continualy of those who were great
> Who never forgot their precious desires
> Hoarded through childhood and remembered from before birth
> Their lips sometimes break into unconscious song
> Their hands sometimes paint
>   Remembering suns that shone before our earth . . .

The poem is still fluid. The second line of this last bit eventually develops into the whole middle section. The doctrine of Platonic reminiscence here skirted becomes at last a leading motif for the first section and is caught up again at the very end of the poem. The great as poets and artists are never again seen so specifically, but persist in the unlocalized splendor of the fourth, fifth, and sixth lines in the completed poem.

Hopkins' "fine desire that fathers thought" cannot here be traced in all the details of its development through this poem. Certain of the major changes, however, may be suggested. For instance, the second draft starts the "sun" expanding into the imagery of flames and fire and burning. It also first grapples with the "blossoming" theme of the beautiful seventh and eighth lines, whose compression is such that its earlier forms must at least be set down in order that its implications may for a moment become explications. The second version has:

Review (Vol. XIII, No. 3). This present essay was written before Spender's article appeared; it has not been changed or modified, since its conclusions, reached on the basis of external evidence, accord with Spender's own account of how he makes a poem.

> They never forgot the most precious desires
> Which blossomed as coral in an orchard
> Which blossomed like coral thick in the spring branches.

Version 3 accepts the first and third lines of the above sketch. Then it refingers the exercise as:

> And   They hoarded from the spring branches thick with coral
> Their merciful desires falling across the body like blossom.

Version 4 arrives at, and version 5 confirms, the final form, which is so much better than its first state not only for its exultant imagery, but for its suggestion that the desires are a precious windfall from some outside power, and for the introduction of the idea of "bodies" which the next section develops.

The third draft first introduces the counterpointed conception of the hostile world that may dull a weak spirit. The lips of the poets are "Never to be blurred over by the sound of traffic." This theme finds its proper place, though not its definitive wording, in the fourth draft:

> Never to allow the noise of . . .

> Never to allow the traffic gradually to smother
> With noise and fog the travail of the spirit.

> Blistering on torrid land

> And to fulfil . . . And to perform the travail of the spirit.

Much of this is crossed out; only as an emendation to the fifth and final draft does "flowering" replace "travail," and echo, at the close of the second section, the "blossoms" that ends the first.

Up to the last draft the poem is fluid. The four lines that open the third section (lines 16-19) persist through earlier

versions, very nearly in their present form, but they top the
page of the third and fourth drafts. The final draft sees them
in their place, articulates the triple division for the first time,
and begins the struggle for right expression in the concluding
four lines. Characteristically, the theme is set at the page-top,
a kind of Work-for-Today:

> Of whom vivid air expresses the peculiar honour
> That, born of the sun, they travelled towards the sun.

This whole battleground should be given, though I cannot
reproduce its interlineations and rejections, as a final glimpse
into a poet's mind when he is at work, and a further proof,
if by now it were needed, that the flowering can only follow
the travail:

The names of those who in their lives fought for life
Who, lovers . . . Who, born of the sun, travelled a short space
    towards the sun
In vibrating . . . For in this vivid air dwells their peculiar honour

Who on vivid air have signed their peculiar honour

That, born of the sun, they travelled towards the sun
Who in vivid air expressed their peculiar honour

That born of the sun they travelled towards the sun.
In vivid air is expressed the peculiar honour

The names of those who in their lives fought for life
And . . . Who seemed to wear at their hearts the flaming centre
Who wore at their hearts fire's . . . the flames . . . fire's vi-
    brating centre.

Born of the sun, they travelled a short while towards the sun
And left the trailing . . . left the vivid air signed with their
    peculiar honour.

Here we must stop. I shall not apologize unduly that the time for viewing these hundred visions and revisions should have occupied us much longer than the taking of a toast and tea, for I believe that such study is rich in rewards, minute and technical as it may seem to those who have time only to read and run, or to run before they read. A poem is a living organism of thought. Its final version is no more than the fiat of its creator that here, now, it possesses its highest, fullest life, ready to be gathered, at last changeless forever, into the artifice of eternity. Its life *as a finished poem* may be realized more fully in the history of its earlier life, in its generating seed, its transmutations, its persistent sap, its buds that withered as well as those that flowered on full branches.

These early sketches are of inestimable value not only for critics and amateurs, but for practicing or ambitious poets as well. Only a poet can teach a poet, even if, as Mr. MacNeice maintains, few of us can truly appropriate even a phrase from the work of the great. Yet I cannot imagine how an energetic tyro—or for that matter, a poet of some maturity and competence—could better spend a month than in turning over such varied manuscripts as are available in the collections of the Lockwood Memorial Library. It is a fair guess that his technique, surety, and inventiveness would all take long jumps ahead. All the secrets of poetic creation need not remain perpetually hidden. The manuscripts at Buffalo would indicate that the old Latin rule might well be emended to read, *Poeta nascitur, atque fit*. Original genius is not dethroned if we recognize, as Dante and Shakespeare recognized, the brotherhood of poets. A guild for the writers of verse might be a most useful union.

Yet how rare are the workshops for poets! In comparison with such poverty, it would seem easy to learn the trade of a sculptor, an architect, a painter, even a musician, through watching a creator at work. But why complain? Such a workshop today exists at Buffalo. Its importance will increase with the years.

This criticism of a poem through studying its origins, signed by its creator as sib and kin, has not been widely practiced. How fascinating and rich, however, has been the experience when the public has been allowed to watch, to participate, as it were, in the creative process! One thinks of how much may be learned by studying the known changes in the works of Wordsworth and Tennyson. Or of the precious manuscripts for Milton and Keats. Or of such books as John Livingston Lowes's *The Road to Xanadu* and James Sutherland's *The Medium of Poetry*. Or of Poe's "The Poetic Principle" and Yeats's letters to Dorothy Wellesley. I would go recklessly further than George Bernard Shaw, if I were a poet; and, not for a preface, but for the worksheets of one of Shakespeare's plays, I would trade half a dozen of his finished products—carefully selected, of course.

Opportunities for studies of this type the Lockwood Library now offers. Let us hope that they will be carried further, there and elsewhere. By this road only can we fully realize that poetry is a great craft and a profession, that the way of the artist aspires toward nobility, transmuting the trivial into the significant, the accidental into the essential, the vague into the clear, the dispirited into the inspiriting, sicknesses and failures and bits of luck and half-wishes and half-thoughts into the permanent forms of beauty. By this road, also, we can realize that the poets travel toward the sun, though it be but for a short while, and leave the vivid air signed with their peculiar honor.

The Meaning
of the Discarded Poem

KARL SHAPIRO

Philomena Andronico

She stands in
the side street
bouncing

a red ball slowly
a little   awk-
wardly hoisting

a red
ball slowly a
little awk-

wardly hoisting
one leg
over. Then

she throws it
############
############

######
following through
with

Typescript worksheet (initial phase)
of "Philomena Andronico" by William Carlos Williams.

Any reaction to stimulus may be causally explained; but the creative act, which is the absolute antithesis of mere reaction, will for ever elude the human understanding.[1]

To C. G. JUNG we are indebted for what must be one of the most discouraging statements concerning the creative activity ever written. I use it as the epigraph to this paper as a suggested motto for the student of manuscripts. If we must enter this ground, let us first abandon hope of making a discovery. Nevertheless, I do not feel that the mystery can be shut up so concisely and finally as the psychologist asserts; and, at any rate, as long as there is poetry there will be curiosity about its genesis. Consider how much more is known today about the behavior of the mind than was known a century ago. Dreams, at least by the initiated, are no longer considered nonsense; may not poems yet be found to express some undiscovered language of the spirit? The current unpopularity of the Freudian contribution to this end is perhaps a symptom of resistance to such a true discovery. We are told by the objectors that if art is a symptom of mental sickness then both its validity as art and its morality must suffer in the eyes of a healthy world. It is also suggested that Freud was a victim of a nineteenth-century delusion that the creative function implies a disability in the creator. Let us look at this argument briefly.

The disability theory, or what I would call the clubfoot theory of art, has by no means been disestablished. Of course, it would be priggish and absurd for the poet to coddle a monster of the mind or to live up to a deformity of the body, although it is common knowledge that these defects are often the mark of the artist. To say they do not exist is to conceal perfectly good evidence. Some effort must still be made to solve the question of sickness and creativity.

We must first understand that by "sick" we really mean

---

[1] C. G. Jung, *Modern Man in Search of a Soul*, Harcourt, Brace, p. 177.

only "different" or what the clinician would call abnormal. What is abnormal is thought to be beyond the needs of nature, or in excess of nature. The sick man finds it necessary to concentrate on some activity in his body or his mind that obliterates all other activities. But "sick" also implies an injury to some part of the body or mind. A child who is in pain because it is cutting a tooth is not said to be sick, as is an adult with an abscessed tooth, the difference being that in one case the pain will be beneficial and in the other malignant. Few people contend that poetry is anything but beneficent, but many believe that the "symptoms" of creation are abnormal, diseased and dangerous. I am not as interested in the outcome of this question as I am in another: whether the artist is more different ("sicker") than, say, a philosopher, a scientist or a man of business. I believe he is, for this reason. It is the nature of the creative mind to familiarize itself with depths of memory, desire, sensation and all the remote quadrants of its being that the speculative or the commercial mind has no need of, and indeed shuns for its own safety. It is certainly true that a great deal—perhaps most—poetry also shuns these subterranean places, and that at a certain level of creativity a poet can compose without seriously ruffling the composure of his spirit. But it is the activity below this level that is most apt to tell us something about itself.

Let us agree, then, that the poet is different from the non-poet in that he makes greater demands on his own Unknown than anyone else, and that he brings to light certain riches which are accorded a universal value. "Rimbaud stole his diamonds, but where?" asks Cocteau. "That is the puzzle."

Anyone who attempts literary criticism must sooner or later come to the point at which he is forced to use terms that designate levels of inspiration, sources of material, kinds of inventiveness, and so on. In general, no effort is made to define these terms, but the reader knows, by the context and from his own experience, what is implied. We are accustomed to find such language as the following in the most scrupulous criticism. "It is only when the ideas become more automatic, come more freely and are less manipulated, that we begin to suspect their origin, to suspect that they spring from a shallower source." [2] The words *ideas, manipulated, origin, shallower source* certainly indicate a theory of composition which we do not know, and do not need to know. This is because it is "our" theory, or what everyone interested in writing thinks is the way writing happens.

The critic's recognition of various levels of creativity points to the existence of a scale or ladder of poetic methods. Just as the expression "a shallower source" indicates other, deeper sources, so are we ultimately led to believe that there is a "top" and a "bottom" to the poetic psyche; and that, if one had insight enough, he could define the functions of the poem-making activity at any level of the scale. It is always interesting to see how these levels are labeled and what functions the investigator attributes to them. Nietzsche, for instance, spoke of the Apollonian, or static principle of art, in distinction to the Dionysian, or dynamic principle, and made the latter stand for the nobler and more life-producing strain.[3] Shelley speaks of the principle of analysis and the principle of synthesis, the first referring to the reason and the second to the imagination. Poetry is a thing of the imagination, although, even at its most glorious, a poem is probably only a pale reflection of the original conception of the poet.[4] Herbert Read uses the terms *organic* and *abstract* to denote a similar correspondence between the truly inventive act and that which represents a fixation of a particular form.[5] Jung discovers a

---

[2] T. S. Eliot, *Selected Essays,* Harcourt, Brace, p. 277.
[3] F. W. Nietzsche, *The Birth of Tragedy.*
[4] P. B. Shelley, *Defence of Poetry.*
[5] Herbert Read, *Form in Modern* Poetry, Sheed and Ward.

dichotomy in the process of artistic creation which he calls the psychological and the visionary modes. The former deals with always intelligible, always familiar material: the resultant art does not disturb the charted currents of the society that sees its birth. Such works, indeed, do not transcend the conscious life of man at all, and it is works of this category that account for the bulk of all literature, music and art. The visionary mode of creation reverses these conditions of composition completely. It is a "primordial experience" from which it derives its power, an experience "foreign and cold, many-sided, demonic and grotesque." The whole process involves a mystic participation in the collective unconscious [6]—and it is there that Jung lets the matter rest.

I would like to mention one more instance of this dualism that crops up when the critic speaks of the origins of poetry, this one the most interesting because, despite its great age, it is the fullest expression of the idea of the double principle of creativity I know of. Speaking of the poet who has no touch of the Muse's madness in his soul, Socrates says, "The sane man disappears and is nowhere when he enters into rivalry with the madman." Madness here is meant as insanity, not as a figurative expression for the creative excitement. What is important in this passage from the *Phaedrus* is that the philosopher makes a distinction between prophecy and madness, including both as aspects of the poetic activity. For the time being, we can use these designations of Plato as the most inclusive we have. *Mantic* or prophetic poetry can stand for the cool, scientific method of creation which relies on fixed rules, signs and traditions to produce its art: *manic* or insane poetry would be that uttered under supernatural suggestion, like the oracles of the Pythoness. One might extend these definitions to include mystical poetry as the highest form of the mantic art—that which makes a direct contact with a deity. We would

[6] C. G. Jung, *op. cit.*

then have a closed circle, the complete circuit, as it were, of the entire poetic process. Socrates takes pains to point out that the "ancients" had only the one word to define both prophecy and madness.

These definitions, of course, would not tell us what happens to the poem after the initial inspiration is given, and, as we shall see in a moment, the poetic material given under supernatural or sub-natural suggestion can scarcely be termed poetry until it has been worked upon by the poet.

I think it would be of value to purely scientific inquiry if poets would now and then try to describe what they felt about the levels of inspiration and the terrain of the poetic psyche. A remarkable letter written by Schiller to a friend who complained of his lack of creative power is quoted by Freud as an example of insight into "freely rising" ideas. It is encouraging to come upon an observation as keen as this:

The reason for your complaint lies, it seems to me, in the constraint which your intellect imposes upon your imagination. . . . Apparently it is not good—and indeed it hinders the creative work of the mind—if the intellect examines too closely the ideas already pouring in, as it were, at the gates. Regarded in isolation, an idea may be quite insignificant, and venturesome in the extreme, but it may acquire importance from an idea which follows it; perhaps, in a certain collocation with other ideas, which may seem equally absurd, it may be capable of furnishing a very serviceable link. The intellect cannot judge all these ideas unless it can retain them until it has considered them in connection with these other ideas. In the case of a creative mind . . . the intellect has withdrawn its watchers from the gates, and the ideas rush in pell-mell, and only then does it review and inspect the multitude. You worthy critics . . . are ashamed or afraid of the momentary and passing madness which is found in all real creators. . . .[7]

[7] S. Freud, "The Method of Dream Interpretation," *Basic Writings of Freud*, Modern Library.

Once again the dualism of the intellect and the imagination is posed, with the characteristic emphasis on madness as the helpmate of poetry.

I would like to give my own impression of the poetic psyche and try to apply this picture to a study of the manuscripts of certain contemporary poets. My impression is based in part on those of the foregoing critics and on my own experience.

The poetic psyche I compare with a tree. To the roots belong the demonic principle, or that which cannot see, but works belowstairs, searching out and down in all directions for anchorage and food. It is probably the first part of the psyche to appear. The trunk and limbs I would identify with the metaphysical principle; this stands in and out of the earth at the same time and is simultaneously interested in being and knowing. The leaves, by far the most populous equipment of the tree, I would identify with the literary principle: only the leaves are millionfold; they flourish, manufacture food and die, some to enrich the earth, most to become dust. Last, the mystical principle, which I would place in the flower, fruit and seed of the tree.

This description, despite its obvious faults, also suggests the biological cycle. When the tree has done its work, our attention is turned to the ground: poetry reproduces itself on the broadest scale by flowering, bearing, and then running to seed. In periods of revolt we are always back to first principles. Now it should not be concluded because of location alone that the demonic principle is inferior to the mystical principle or that one extreme stands for evil and the other for good. The most we can say about the two extremes of the poetic psyche is that in the demonic principle the poetic material arrives, whereas in the mystical principle it is arrived at. The one begins in frenzy, the other achieves frenzy. And about the relative greatness of these four principles, I think it would be unsafe to say anything more than that the greatest poets use several or all four of the principles, in turn or together. Jung, in keeping with his definition of the visionary art, cites three works as among the highest examples, *The Divine Comedy*, the second part of Goethe's *Faust*, and *The Shepherd of Hermas*.[8] * The first two I would place among the foremost poems, that is, those that duplicate the life-cycle of the tree, but the third, which is a work of literature only by assumption, I would not include at all. Plato's differentiation of prophetic from poetic madness is useful here. I cannot believe that apocalyptic literature is poetry, if poetry is to have any meaning of its own. This is not a quibble; *The Shepherd of Hermas* is part of the primitive Christian literature almost included in the final *New Testament*. As such, it is free of the strictures of literary aims.

The question now rises, when do we know who is a true demonic or mystical poet and who is not. What is the difference, say, between the mysticism of Gerard Manley Hopkins and that of Augustus Montague Toplady? Or what is the difference between the demonism of Arthur Rimbaud and that of André Breton? Is vision enough or must we have the fruit of the vision in terms of poetry? Is madness enough or must we have the poem that emerges from the frenzy? Merely to write about heaven or hell is insufficient, if the writing lacks the intuitive genius of form. And merely to be mad or prophetic is not enough, unless the madness or the mysticism be of the prophetic variety. There is no good surrealist poetry because surrealism merely imitates the conditions of madness; because it violates the genius of form by trying to make form insane! Compare such a technique with that of a true demonic poet, Rimbaud or Poe, who is almost classical in his craftsmanship. Notice also that the majority

[8] C. G. Jung, *op. cit.* * Jung, however, is speaking of vision and not of poetry.

of English hymns are inferior and even abominable poems. The same is true of national anthems, political verse, and other hortatory branches of the art.—We need not look to the asylum or the monastery for poetry.

Literary poetry, the bulk of all poetry that lies between the blossoms and the roots, escapes analysis for hidden elements; by and large, it is simply human poetry, full of the foibles and tricks of wit that belong to wide-awake life. But frequently we come upon the poet who gravitates toward mysticism or toward the depths, but who nevertheless does not quite rise from the literary foliage. I think two such poets are Yeats and Rilke; both seem to possess everything except the conviction of their own visions, and almost deliberately they give us the impression of make-believe. Hart Crane, one of the poets whose manuscripts I want to discuss, suffered the opposite fate. Crane was that rare thing, a true demonic poet, who, when his demon deserted him, failed into wretched literary pretense.

It seems, then, that the final test of validity, the final means of discovering the level of inspiration of a particular poet, lies nowhere but in the form. And if that is so, we are back where we started from—as Jung threatened. There is nothing to do but try to break through the poem from another side. We have seen that conviction (vision or madness) does not count for much when it comes to producing a good poem, for if that were so, the greatest sufferers and the greatest visionaries would be the greatest poets. We have seen also that the will to be a poet doesn't count for much either. For to vision or madness or the poetic desire must be added the indispensable element of the knowledge of form. *Genius in poetry is probably only the intuitive knowledge of form.* The dictionary contains all words and a textbook on verse contains all meters, but nothing can tell the poet which words to choose and in what rhythms to let them fall except his own intuitive knowledge of form. It is thus that form, or style, to use the more common term, becomes the instrument of interpretation and the measure of the poet's gift. Form, indeed, must override any other consideration in the criterion of the true poem. The form is the intelligence of the poem, and upon the form hangs the very life of the poem.—One might add, parenthetically, that a great quantity of literary criticism today overlooks this tenet, with the result that inferior works are judged side by side with the best on the grounds that both have "just as much to say." This practice, I think, will eventually invalidate a whole corpus of our criticism.

Can the study of form under construction give evidence of the level of inspiration on which the poet stands at the time he composes a particular work? Or is the final evidence the finished work, in which so many of our clues are buried? I think we are now constrained to use the former method if we are to storm the gates at all, for even experts admit defeat in the other field. What we must do is to tear the poem down, unless we are fortunate enough to have rescued the records of its creation. From working-drafts, marginalia, personalia, and the like, we can proceed to the external form (psychology of imagery), to the materials of form (language and metric), to the sources of form (personality, tradition and the Unknown). We will then be as close to the place of the creative act as we can hope to get. In the case of the literary poem we can probably learn no more than the particular psychology of imagery, but we do not expect this kind of poem to conceal anything from our view. The literary poem is written off the top of one's head, as the humorous saying goes. But the poem of any of the other levels might well reveal that concealable material which will lead to the portals of discovery.

Before examining the manuscripts I would like to make one further observation about the peculiarities of this kind of research. In many cases the most difficult preliminary stages of composition seem to have been accomplished mentally, that is, without the poet's knowledge of how many trials and errors he has overcome before his pen has touched paper. The habitual poet perhaps has learned a technique of discard of which he is no longer aware. Therefore much valuable material will always be missing from the record. During the progress of the poem we often come upon a "semi-final" version of a verse or stanza which is so inferior to the final version that any question of establishing the relationship seems impossible. These are probably moments of the greatest importance to the poet and to us.

STUDY OF *The Express*, BY STEPHEN SPENDER

The author at the time of composition is a young man with certain identifiable ideas about progress, justice, and social change. He is, however, a poet and an optimist who is making a search in himself for a new iconography which will implement his poetry as well as the beliefs he has adopted. Alternately he is tossed up to heights of happiness by his optimism and his poetic genius, and thrown down into despondency by his "social" despair and his inability to assist in the rebirth. Like Whitman, another poet with a sweeping political philosophy, he fuses the love of comrades with a personal eros, and saturates his verses with symbols of masculinity. One interpretation of *The Express* must suggest the masculine image of sexuality, as one interpretation of *The Landscape Near an Aerodrome* must suggest the opposite, the destroyed image of feminine creativity, with its ikons of grief-stricken women, and the church. The more conscious stimulus which would evoke the theme of the poem about the train is the barely latent idea of progress and change, with its corollary idea of escape ("further than Edinburgh or Rome"). The overt theme, of course, is praise of the beauty of this machine and the ecstasy of its motion.

There are in the Lockwood Library's Spender notebook six sequential, incremented versions, which may be called drafts A, B, C, D, E, and F. The initial draft is almost the completed poem in itself, except for the four final moving verses which lift the express from the rails and plunge it into a garden of night-sky, birdsong and boughs. But there is a good deal of interference before this transitional miracle can be effected. The opening lines of this draft contain minor textual changes and two possibly significant ones. (By a minor change I mean one that moves only a negligible distance toward a different level. Thus "the clear statement of pistons" in becoming "the black statement of pistons" merely clarifies the metaphor of "plain manifesto." A plain manifesto makes a clear statement, but a plain manifesto, to put it in headlines, makes a black statement. It is extraordinary that in Spender's crowded imagery there is never any sense of confusion, even, as I shall try to show, when he switches abruptly from the physical to the mystical image.)

Here is the opening of the first draft:

> After the first powerful plain manifesto,
> The ~~clear~~ statement of pistons, without more fuss
>   black
> But gliding like a queen she leaves the station:

The first significant change is not actually a change at all, but an obliterated word (completely indecipherable) between "queen" and "she." I take it that the poet here is disturbed by the word "queen," which used in this particular meliorative connection puts up a warning signal in his mind. "Queen" is not very good socialism, and it must be remembered that Spender is forging an appropriate language as he writes. But more than this, the word probably raises the strange question

of the sex of trains. The vehicle in the poem, with its black-
ness, iron, bolts, pistons and power, argues for the male interpretation. The wheels, flight, song, "luminous self-possession,"
mystery, and of course the analogy of ships at sea, argue for
the feminine interpretation. Also a decision becomes important because of the eleven subsequent *she*'s and *her*'s, which
would have to become *he*'s and *his*'s. The original impulse
to make the symbol feminine Spender finds correct, and the
poem acquires a pleasing dualism at the outset.

The second significant change occurs in the imagery of the
cemetery, through which the express passes. Draft A stands:

> Without bowing and with restrained unconcern
> She notices the houses humbly crowding outside
> And then the gasworks and at last the printed psalm
> Of death written by gravestones in the cemetery.

Draft B makes the final alterations:

> Without bowing and with restrained unconcern
> She passes the houses which humbly crowd outside,
> The gasworks, and at last the heavy page
> Of death printed by gravestones in the cemetery.

"Psalm" is the undesirable word here. Spender's whole conception of death at this period is given very full treatment in
The Funeral, which we will examine in a moment. In keeping with the imagery of the manifesto, printing and change,
the psalm is altered to "the heavy page of death," that is to
say, a mere statement of death, without religious overtones.
This consistency of aim contributes to the enormous force in
the poem.

A third change is of possible interest. The express is now in
open country and

> It is now she begins to sing—at first quite low
> And then loud and at last with a jazzy madness—

"With a jazzy madness" stood originally as "with mad joy," a phrase almost devoid of tone. The substitution of "jazzy" with its good-bad (modern-decadent) associations is a piece of extreme cleverness, and in a sense would be the turning-point of the poem, or a lead to the departure of the train into the soft ecstasy of the closing lines: but it is still too early for that. There is this one seductive suggestion of the slattern and then a quick tightening "of tunnels, of brakes, of innumerable bolts." It is not yet time to leave the train.

Another brilliant minor change occurs in the development of the verses:

> And always light, aerial, under~~neath~~ this
> Is the tapping metre of her wheels. (*Draft A*)

Draft C reads:

> And always light, aerial, underneath
>   racing
> Is (Goes) the ~~tapping~~ metre of her wheels.

which emerges in Draft D in the final form:

> And always light, aerial, underneath
>   elate
> Goes the ~~racing~~ metre of her wheels.

Here again the perfect solution has been found to describe sensorially and emotionally the condition of the train at top speed. By repeating the word "elate" by itself very rapidly one even awakens in the ear the characteristic music of the train.

The poem, according to Draft C, is now at the half-way mark. The express has been put into full speed, and the poet's problem is what to do with it. There are two possible directions the express can take: one toward the poet, down, as it were, toward the depths of his psyche; and up, away from the poet and people, into the night of comet, flame and the

bodiless world of the spirit. Some such struggle is evident in
the following Drafts C and D, which should be shown in full.
Draft C:

After the first powerful plain manifestoe
The black statement of pistons, without more fuss
But gliding like a queen, she leaves the station.
Without bowing and with restrained unconcern
She passes the houses which humbly crowd outside,
The gasworks, and at last the heavy page
Of death printed by gravestones in the cemetery.
Beyond the town there lies the open country
Where, gathering speed, she acquires mystery,

                       at
The luminous self-possession of ships ~~on~~ ocean.
It is now she begins to sing—at first quite low,
~~And~~ Then loud, and at last with a jazzy madness—
The song of her whistle screaming at corners,
Of ~~blindi~~ deafening tunnels, brakes, innumerable bolts;
And always light, aerial, underneath .

         racing
Is (Goes) the ~~tapping~~ metre of her wheels.
Her passengers   (further than Edinburgh or Rome)
Explore new eras of wild happiness
At night when dark flags ~~touch the glass~~ knock the glass
And only the low stream-line brightness
Of moonlight on the tossing hills is white.

Rapt in what
~~Entranced by a~~ symphony (ies) they dream

    tapping
Of ~~gleaming~~ metals: and sharp strange shapes entrance

              lines
Them in their rigid ~~folds.~~ Not bird song, no nor bough
Breaking with honeyed buds, nor dreams of India

  hunting   jeweled
And ~~tracing~~ through thick leaves the ~~rare jewelled~~ tiger,
So rules with stamped and iron image ~~Can build~~
The strange world where they turn, as this
Of jetting steam and rods . / . She stops

In Draft D the first ten lines remain unaltered. Then:

It is now she begins to sing—at first quite low
Then loud and at last with a jazzy madness—
The song of her whistle screaming at corners,
Of deafening tunnels, brakes, innumerable bolts:
And always light, aerial, underneath
       elate
Goes the ~~racing~~ metre of her wheels.
Her passengers, (further than Edinburgh or Rome),
Explore new eras of wild happiness
At night when dark flags knock the glass
And only the low stream-line brightness
Of moonlight on the tossing hills is white
~~Oh,~~ They are wrapt in music no bird song nor bough
Breaking with honey buds, nor tale from India
~~Of~~ hunting through dripping boughs the precious tiger,
  Can build   *iron*
~~Creates~~   ~~They are~~ ruled round with lines
                    builds
~~And stamped with imagery which makes new worlds:~~
~~This strange new world~~
And strange new forms of rods and jets of steam
Stamp on their brains an image of new worlds
~~Their brains are stamped pressed on by with forms poured~~
    ~~on by steam~~
They watch
The images of power stamp their brain
~~And of works whose fires~~
~~And of metals moulten to create new works worlds~~
And hear

      Ruled round with iron lines
They watch the images of power that stamp their brain
Impressed by thunder of waters & tearing steam
And roar of furnace(s) that mould machines.

It is probably the idea of travelers and passengers that awakens the complexity of dark associations in the poet's mind, and as we shall see, it is only by eliminating people altogether that unity is maintained in the poem, and the express freed to establish itself in the cosmos. Meanwhile the poem is beset with active and malignantly beautiful objects, dark gusts, flags of wind that knock the glass, dreams of India, and a jeweled tiger. Rapt in symphonies, the mind begins to dream, then awakens, for the dreams become tales.—The question is how this irrelevant material got as far as these two versions of the poem, and what this material signifies. I will attempt a guess. "And tracing through thick leaves the rare jeweled tiger" and "of hunting through dripping boughs the precious tiger" are not even Spenderian images. In poem 13, however, of Spender's first published book, we come upon something of interest:

> I feared more than tigers their muscles like iron
> And their jerking hands and knees tight on my arms . . .
> They were light, they sprang out behind hedges . . .

The poet is here speaking of children "who were rough." Again,

> We lacked the Spring-like resources of the tiger.

which comes from a political poem in which the poet begs that the future will never say that Spender's generation lacked the resources to build a new world. Without knowing the sequence of composition of the three poems it is possible to see that the rough boys who sprang out at the boy Spender like tigers have a dual significance. They hunted him and yet he chooses to identify himself with them; he is the hunter and the hunted at once. The rare jeweled tiger, the precious tiger, the tiger with Spring-like resources (the pun is self-explanatory) is possibly Spender's hound of heaven.

There is one further problem of the transit of Spender's symbol of the express which I do not know where to locate. It occurs in the seemingly child-like verse "At last, further than Edinburgh or Rome" and occurs in all six drafts of the poem. The only thing I am sure of here is that the names are not simply place-names. The obvious connections would be Edinburgh, the actual destination of the train (?) and Rome, the past. But in examining the verses that immediately follow the six Edinburgh and Rome configurations, it seems that the names are only a springboard for the final destination of the express and the poem, namely, "beyond the crest of the world" where both train and poem reach the destination "night." This establishes the resolution of the poem; the express is to be merged in darkness, in flame, in song, in boughs breaking with honey buds.

> Ah, like a comet through flame, she moves entranced
> Wrapped in her music no bird song, no, nor bough
> Breaking with honey buds shall ever equal.

The mystical melting together of sight, sound and smell in these verses dispels the jazzy madness, the mechanical elate meter of wheels, and leaves us in a trance of excitement that is happy and acceptable.

STUDY OF *The Funeral*, BY STEPHEN SPENDER

The second Spender poem I want to examine is *The Funeral*, which bears some relationship to *The Express* and does, in fact, directly precede it in the first published edition. In the notebook it occupies two pages and consists of two versions, the first incomplete, the second virtually finished. A moral consideration of the poem is out of place here, but it would be of help to remember that this work pleads an extreme case in an extreme manner, and pursues its point to a mercilessly logical conclusion. The argument is that grief for death is dead. A worker has passed away, but one who has given his life for the "hive" (the state). Therefore rejoice;

read lists of projects for building over his grave, and be thankful for what this man contributed. A deleted line at the top of the second draft reads, "No more are they haunted by the individual grief." *Haunted* I think is the real key in which the poem is written.

In the initial quatrain of the first draft we get a preliminary exercise of thought which is absent in *The Express* manuscript.

On the little hill at the edge of the town
They stand amongst stiff grass and the breeze lifts their hair,
The strange cause of rejoicing that lightens their eyes
Is the death of a hero of labour.

This preparatory work the poet finds unsatisfactory. It is too obvious, too sentimental, despite the curious theme it announces. The weakness of this beginning nevertheless leads immediately into the almost final and very arresting opening

For death is ~~only~~ another milestone on their way

In the second draft the weak quatrain is obliterated and the conjunctive "for" free to drop out.

Death is another milestone on their way

is a typically powerful Spenderian beginning. But, for the moment, it is the rejected material that is of interest. First, there is the setting of the poem, the locale, which a few stanzas down we learn is London! Second, there is the time, which from "the little hill" phrase I would adduce to be soon, just after the world revolution. The little hill presumably denotes a little cemetery, a new one, not one of those infinite, hideous and sprawling affairs where the pre-revolutionary dead are buried. Finally, we are made to know that instead of grief there is rejoicing; the poet still finds this "strange," for everything has become different quite suddenly.

In the succeeding quatrain the poet discusses with himself the relative merits of jobs in the new world—or so it seems from the change in the text. The hero "excelled all others in making, say, driving belts." "Say" is eventually thought superfluous, as is the moral question for which it stands. Both the verse and the argument are strengthened by this simple deletion. The stanza shows numerous textual revisions, mostly pertinent to the political meaning of the poem.

For death is ~~the last~~ festivity; it is the time for statistics

When they record how much ~~this~~ one atom contributed ~~to the state,~~

They ~~laugh as we~~ are glad as they lay ~~him back~~ him in the earth ~~from which~~ whence he came
And thank him for what he gave them.

Stanza four is the "London" stanza and is of interest because it expresses what is *exactly* in the poet's mind, but not what will help create the poem.

Then follow the speeches and the songs of the new life
And lists are read out of projects to build ~~new~~ steel-works
And to pull down
The worst of the slums around London.

"Steel-works" falls by the way in the next version and becomes "projects for building." In steel-works we sense a militancy to which the poet probably objects. (There is now no further need of militancy; we are in the immediate future, but we are already safe. "The worst of the slums around London" becomes "The last of the slums around London.")

The fifth quatrain ends this version, and the poem is begun again "on the little hill at the edge of the town." It now proceeds smoothly, almost finally, through all its seven quatrains, the first and fourth of which are later struck out. Both of these are local, political stanzas; poetically they bear no relationship to the rest of the poem, but are rather the stimuli that excite the creation in its development. The closing stanza, the most exciting of all, appears in the second version in finished form.

No more are they haunted by the individual grief
Nor the crocodile tears of European genius
The decline of a culture
Mourned by scholars who dream of the ghosts of Greek boys.

This is the only moment when one feels a tremor of motion below the surface of the poem; until this final quatrain we are standing in the near future. Then the sudden look behind into the present. I have never been sure what is meant by "the crocodile tears of European genius" though probably it has a political meaning for the initiated. At any rate, this quatrain is the only one that *appeared* without having to undergo development. Can we presume from this that it is the "inspired" stanza, or that it contains the real substance of the poem? If so, what does it mean and what light does it throw on the rest of the creation? Probably only this. That Spender at this period experiences the individual grief and is haunted by it; it is the one thing he must submerge in order to become a better socialist and a more effective revolutionary. *He* is the individual grief upon which his scorn is showered. In other works in this collection Spender constantly makes it clear that he is not "using" his revolutionary material for his own "singing-tree" (his own aims). No doubt it is the enthusiasm of the political visionary that enables him to dismiss the heritage of European genius with such finality. Everything must go, what is held most dear, even oneself.

The Funeral carries a tremendous shock in its quiet lines. What in the notebook threatens to become merely a piece of boyish pettishness, turns out to be a brilliant experiment in nihilism. Anyone who has followed Spender's poetry closely will have recognized an integral struggle between himself and his idea of justice, a struggle I think that is between Spender's mysticism and his socialism. The poems about Beethoven and the truly great do not spring from the same psyche as the poems about comrades and the need for destruction. The direction of the express train is not accidental but is a symptom of this poet's psychical direction. There is, in fact, a sizeable mystical vocabulary in Spender, which is most of the time overlooked but is now and then miscalled "romantic." "As iron heated red hot loses its own appearance and glows like fire" is a typical Spenderian form; it was written, however, by St. Bernard. Spender is a first-rate language maker, and it is therefore doubly interesting to notice the ease with which he draws upon the vocabulary of the ecstatics. "Cross, rose, pilgrimage, missionary, love, wheel, death, distance, the mystic One, heaven, peace, trumpeter, sun, spirit, edge of being, moth, worms," and others, taken out of context would not appear to rise from the Spenderian vocabulary. Some of the same words used by Ycats, for example, would carry only a literary force or a pseudo-mystical beauty. Spender's mysticism, it can be argued, must be real because he has to fight it back and because he has to find a weapon, political materialism, with which to render it harmless. In his hand that weapon itself grows flowers, in the manner of an ancient miracle.

STUDY OF *Philomena Andronico* BY WILLIAM
CARLOS WILLIAMS

The following poem has never appeared in a book, and I assume it is the poet's purpose to leave it only for a study of this kind. Its worksheets consist of fifteen typed pages corrected in pencil; they present, in all, five versions. As a discarded William Carlos Williams piece, I think nevertheless that it throws some light on his *pratique* as well as on his particular poetic aims. In Williams, as in Wallace Stevens to a lesser extent, we have the ultimate development of form that seeks to arrest or still the image. This is not to say that motion and action are dispensed with in this method, but that, even when the subject matter is of a very violent nature, as is often the case with Williams, the extreme surface of the poem remains or attempts to remain at a dead calm. It is a poetry as closely allied to painting as any I know.

Readers who sometimes search for the logical word sequence in Williams are baffled at what seems a jumble of things set down without normal language relationships. What is good to remember in reading Williams is that the words, or at least the key words, are very like ideographs, or symbols of the objects thought of. Ordinarily we do not call to mind the object or attribute for which a word stands; the word itself is enough to satisfy our desire for a meaning. In Williams the objects themselves all but spring up before our eyes, and it is the logic of these almost-objects in careful arrangement that provides the narrative of ideas.

The poem is named *Philomena Andronico,* and from the context we learn that a little (immigrant?) girl is bouncing a ball. That is all the subject matter we have. Here is what seems to be the penultimate version of the manuscript: *

> With the boys busy
> at ball
> in the worn lot
> nearby
>
> She stands in
> the short street
> reflectively bouncing
> the red ball

* It is interesting to notice that in Williams a change may involve only the typographical position of a word or a phrase.

Slowly
practiced
a little awkwardly
throwing one leg over

not as she had done
formerly
screaming and
missing

but slowly
surely and then
pausing first
she throws the ball

with a full slow
very slow
and easy motion
following through

with a slow
half turn
as the ball flies
and rolls gently

at the child's feet
~~waiting beyond~~
and yet he misses
it and turns

and runs while she
slowly regains
her former
pose

        the
then/ runs ~~her~~ fingers
of one hand
up through
her loose short hair,
~~the quickly~~

       leans ⸝her
to draws ~~one~~ stocking
tight and then
~~the other~~
~~waiting~~

in the warm still
air

and tilts
her hip
and lets her arms
fall loosely
(waiting) at her sides

This poem, as I say, is the ABC of Williams' technique. Nothing half so simple appears in any of his published work, most of which is as formally complex as this is elementary. We are lucky to find only the essentials of a Williams poem; in this case at least we are free to discuss only the color and the development of the ideographs. The poem is a study in the control of the objects it deals with and the deceleration of their motions.

In Draft A the word "busy" first comes under observation and is struck out. The second draft eliminates the first stanza entirely, only to pick it up in the third version, but without "busy" again. The fourth version restores the troublesome word, and it survives in the fifth and final forms. This particular problem is not peculiar to Williams, however, but to all poets. It merely questions a possibly inappropriate adjective. The next problem is of a different nature.

The "meter" in a visual poem of this kind is determined by spacing and by creating a mental stop or advance with the use of the appearance of the words, their groupings. Thus Version A reads:

> She stands in
> the side street
> bouncing
>
> a red ball slowly *or* a red
>   ball slowly a

Version B reads:

> she stands in
> the side street/
> bouncing a red
>
> ball slowly

Version C repeats B, and D inserts a decelerating adverb:

> she stands in
> the side street
> ~~reflectively~~
> bouncing a red ball
>
> slowly

which, like "busy" is first doubted and finally accepted. The semi-final version:

> She stands in
> the short street
> reflectively/ bouncing
> a ~~the~~ red ball
>
> Slowly

introduces the further change "the short street," which again defines a space. The final draft of the manuscript:

> She stands in
> the short street
> reflectively bouncing
> the red ball
>
> Slowly

definitely fixes the pace of the poem, which nevertheless tends to speed up. The words "slow," "slowly," and "very slow" occur six times in the course of the poem. Other brakes are "reflectively," "surely," "pausing," "easy motion," "gently," "former pose," "half turn," "waiting," "still air." The word "quickly" is struck out in the semi-final draft—I should suppose quickly, were it not that it had persisted through so many versions.

Throughout the evolution of the poem as much attention is given to the spacing of unchanged words and groups of words as to the internal changes themselves. These are as varied and as numerous as occur in the worksheets of a Spender poem but are even more difficult to follow because we know so little of the medium and cannot follow the method of selection as clearly.

Certain other word configurations in the poem are extremely piquant. They seem to add another dimension to the picture, without indicating how. Philomena stands in the side street (Draft B) bouncing a red ball and hoisting one leg:

> over not as
> formerly screaming
> and missing

"Formerly" could be a moment ago (the moment before the poem) or a year ago, a recollection from the poet's past. "Screaming" (with vexation?) does not help qualify the image. The odd use of the word "yet" is another delicate reference to some hidden emotion in the observer.

> the ball flies
> and rolls
> gently at the child's
>
> feet and yet he
> misses it and

I think "yet" is intended to convey a suggestion of uneasiness and to create an interference in the reader's mind.

Judging this composition in the light of Williams' more intricate work, I think any conclusion would be risky except this. The poet's emotions, ideas, and sensations are selected and tranquilized in the eye; then distributed on paper as ideographs, and finally arranged, as an artist arranges the elements in a picture. The surface tension of this poetry is so great that it seems impossible for submerged material to break through, or for the reader to see down through the exterior.

STUDY OF *Cape Hatteras* BY HART CRANE

Everything about Hart Crane points to the poet possessed, the man in the grip of the demon. Three of his poetic ancestors, Poe, Baudelaire and Rimbaud, belong to the deepest mines of the poetic psyche; the fourth, Walt Whitman, presented him with the false vision of life which eventually Crane was to employ for his own self-destruction. Crane's instinct was for the depths, but through circumstance and innocence this instinct was translated into the will to die. His early work takes place aboveground; he will pause long enough to be hypnotized by the shine of white buildings.

> As silent as a mirror is believed
> Realities plunge in silence by. . . .

> I am not ready for repentance;

When finally he is ready for repentance (the descent into the depths?) it will be too late to save himself. He has been shown a false mythology in a mirror, and plunging after it he will die. *Ce ne peut être la fin du monde, en avançant,* is the menacing superscription at the beginning of his first book. Narcissus is willing to plunge into the mirror; at any rate, he has caught a vision of his destiny. But between the journey and the suicide lies the heart-breaking road of disenchantment. At last the myth falls apart before his eyes, and the disappointmnt is too great to live with.

By the time the poet has come to write the *Cape Hatteras* segment of his epic, he already knows the futility of the poem. It is not only the weakest link in *The Bridge;* its inspiration, a kind of hymn to Whitman, threatens to poison the whole work.

Friends of Crane encouraged the poet to work over this section of *The Bridge* after it had advanced as far as the version I am going to discuss. Between this version * and the final form there must have been other worksheets; there are even differences between the Paris edition and the first American edition. Crane's method of composition kept him at work on a poem as long as it was available for improvement.

The majority of changes are external minor alterations made in the interest of a tighter meter or a more effective image.

> Imponderable the dinosaur who
> sinks slow,

in which the "who" is dropped. Or

> Or to recount the priests' march through Bombay—

becomes, without altering the number of syllables, a more exact description:

> Or how the priests walked—slowly through Bombay—

The internal changes, even in this advanced draft, are often of the greatest import. A comparison of the changes in the second stanza discloses a deepening of the image.

* The *Cape Hatteras* manuscript is not the property of the Lockwood Library, but is quoted here with the permission of its owner, Peter Blume.

To that deep wonderment, our native clay,
Whose depth of red, eternal flesh of Pocahontas—
Those continental folded aeons, surcharged
With sweetness below derricks, chimneys, tunnels,
Is veined of that eternity that's pledged us . . .
While overhead, like corkscrew squeaks of radio static
The captured fume of space forms in the ears,
What whisperings of far lookouts on the main
Relapsing into silence . . . Time annuls—
Time, the serpent, retrieves the telescope,
Constricts it to its primal nest of vertigos,
The labyrinth, compressible, of our own egos.

Compare the final form.

To that deep wonderment, our native clay
Whose depth of red, eternal flesh of Pocahontus—
Those continental folded aeons, surcharged
With sweetness below derricks, chimneys, tunnels—
Is veined by all that time has really pledged us . . .
And from above, thin squeaks of radio static,
The captured fume of space foams in our ears—
What whisperings of far watches on the main
Relapsing into silence, while time clears
Our lenses, lifts a focus, resurrects
A periscope to glimpse what joys or pain
Our eyes can share or answer—then deflects
Us, shunting to a labyrinth submersed
Where each sees only his dim past reversed . . .

These turgid verses in the first form are trying, as it were, to end the poem. The serpent Time takes back the telescope, collapses it to the primal eye, the pool of our own egos. But this is too sudden for the poet, and he gives Time back the telescope while she clears the lenses and resurrects—a periscope. The meaning of this sleight-of-hand may lie in the "labyrinth submersed" which Crane presumably would like to reach. "The darkening pool" in the following stanza becomes "the lucid pool," a change, if changes mean anything at all, that is a rather desperate one. The fatal image of the mirror is again to the fore.

Left Hesperus mirrored in the lucid pool.

The poetry now becomes reckless, leaving the sea for the air, the submarine for the airplane.

Dream cancels dream in this new realm of fact
From which we wake into the dream of act;
Seeing himself an atom in a shroud—
Man hears himself an engine in a cloud!

"Hearing himself a locomotive in a cloud!" is the first attempt. The poet does not succeed in assimilating this machine imagery, as is his aim, but instead gives us a burlesque Blakian line. The succeeding stanza invokes Walt Whitman, and what is equally interesting, a sudden wraith, the spirit that portends the death of the watcher. The wraith does not appear except in the printed version. The poet asks Whitman if infinity

Be still the same as when you walked the beach
Near Paumanok—your lone patrol—and heard the wraith
Through surf, its bird note there a long time falling . . .

The wraith might not be so prophetic after all, were it not for what follows. As in the tunnel, where Crane meets the demonic eyes of Poe—like agate lanterns—here the poet is pursued by the eyes of Whitman, which appear in the cliffs of Wall Street and "back over Connecticut pastures," but chiefly in the sea.

Sea eyes and tidal, undenying, bright with myth!

It is as illuminating a line as the poet has written about himself and his apprehensions. It seems to rise from the same deeps as another poem about a drowned father which sings of "the pearls that were his eyes."

The following stanza is the well-known paean to machinery which begins "The nasal whine of power whips a new universe." It is not Crane at his best by any means, but it throws light on his curious method of composing, or rather bears out the connection of *artificial stimulation* and poetry in Crane's case. The poet's biographer records that Crane would sit at his desk with a jug of wine and a victrola going full blast, often repeating the same jazzy tune again and again.[9] Horton believes that the visionary fervor which Crane achieved by means of such stimuli could not have been awakened without some such agitation of the senses. Both music and liquor eventually became identified in Crane's mind with the process of composition. It is also recorded that the poet derived giddy and half-drunken sensations from machine noises, machine shapes, and the gigantic motions of machines. "Power's script,—wound, bobbin-bound, refined— / Is stropped to the slap of belts on booming spools, spurred / Into the bulging bouillon, harnessed jelly of the stars." This crude and unworked poetry gives some idea of what he must have experienced before the demon of the machine.

Following the machine passage there comes a long dizzying adventure of the airplane. Two further images of sea-death disappear from the printed version of the poem. The draft reads:

Two brothers in a twinship left the dune, the glazed lagoon,—

the final phrase being omitted from the book.

Seductions blue and schedules rife of doom!

becomes

To what fierce schedules, rife of doom apace!

[9] Philip Horton, *Hart Crane, The Life of an American Poet*, Norton.

The Wright brothers' theme leads into an excited vision of aerial warfare. In some manner this battle is telescoped into the *Cape Hatteras* theme, the purpose being to unify the poem as much as possible. The draft version shows a large number of minor differences, and at least one of interest. The draft reads:

O bright circumferences, heights employed to lift
War's fiery kennel, interpolated red in vaporous offings:

which develops into

O bright circumferences, heights employed to fly
War's fiery kennel masked in downy offings,—

Nothing is gained, however. The poem is too far disrupted at this stage to achieve unity.

Two stanzas down we come upon an unintelligible reference to Sanskrit.

Remember, Falcon-Eye,
Thou hast a Sanscrit in thy sailor wrist, a charge
To conjugate infinity's far verb anew . . . !

The printed version

Remember, Falcon-Ace,
Thou hast there in thy wrist a Sanskrit charge
To conjugate infinity's dim marge—
Anew . . . !

hardly clears up the puzzle, which might serve as reference to the inscrutability of the text as itself.

It will be useful to transcribe the original of the next passage that invokes Whitman, because it clarifies Crane's intent in the poem better than the finished version.

But who has better held the heights than thou,
O Walt?—Ascensions that bespeak in my own veins

Thee at the junction elegiac, there, of speed
With blank eternity. And thou dost wield the rebound seed.
The inescapable equation there beyond, below
The competent grass, the probable loam. O Walt,
We wait, some of us, on the sand the ultimate frontier
Not wings, but rhythm possible of wings!) . . .
And thou shalt bide us there beyond our fall.
For who was he but thou, who undertook the plunge,
O carrier-creator of song's breakless chain!

The indigestible idea of Whitman as the carrier-creator who
undertook the plunge drops from the revision, which in other
respects also shows enormous improvement.

The stars have grooved our eyes with old persuasions
Of love and hatred, birth,—surcease of nations . . .
But who has held the heights more sure than thou,
O Walt!—Ascensions of thee hover in me now
As thou at junctions elegiac, there, of speed
With vast eternity, dost wield the rebound seed!
The competent loam, the probable grass,—travail
Of tides awash the pedestal of Everest, fail
Not less than thou in pure impulse inbred
To answer deepest soundings! O, upward from the dead
Thou bringest tally, and a pact, new bound
Of living brotherhood!

With more relevancy, Whitman is invoked as the spirit of the
Mourner who has kept account of the wounds of armies from
Appomattox to Somme. By now Crane has a binding thread
of the tradition which he believes links him to Whitman, his
Meistersinger. From here to the end of the poem there are
virtually no changes of any kind, textual or otherwise. Either
the poet has abandoned the poem or he feels that he has accomplished finality in the version. The ending of the poem is
neither better nor worse than the rest of it: it is merely a little
clearer.

Only so much can be said of the *Cape Hatteras* poem, in the draft and in the printed form. Unlike other sections of *The Bridge*, with the exception of the sentimental "Indiana," it is a piece of poorly conceived and poorly articulated work. That it foreshadows the poet's death is of course highly conjectural, but that it discusses some means and aspects of death in rapid sequence makes it possible for us to say that Crane at this time had already come face to face with his destiny. We do know that when the poet was writing *Cape Hatteras* he had lost the confidence of his vision; his personality was already disintegrating, but his talent proved itself at least once more in his last Mexican poem, *The Broken Tower*. The maudlin conclusion of *Cape Hatteras*, hand in hand with Walt, under a rainbow, is the defeated cry of a demonic poet who has lost his way. It is not the cry of a man who has lost his gift, which was the weak construction Crane chose to put upon his dilemma.

SUMMARY

We should now be in a position to make some tentative conclusions about our findings. Have we demonstrated anything of interest or importance, or have we merely added to the vocabulary of critical slang? Is there any meaning to the discarded poem beyond what is already known? Is the door to the principle of creativity still closed?

To the last question we can answer yes, though still without involving ourselves in Jung's discouraging postulate. To the others we can make the following summary:

1. Literary, or wide-awake poetry is the poetry of reaction, in Jung's sense of the word. Given the necessary biographical data we should be able to make a complete analysis of its formation. But the poetry of the extremes, being the antithesis of mere reaction, must be pure stimulus in itself. The data of biography are here useless.

2. The creative activity is a "sickness" insofar as it is injurious to some other activity of the psyche. That definition, however, is of interest only to the doctor and the police. Where the consideration is the poetry, we must assume that the poet allows certain activities of his psyche to degenerate. The good poet who is a good specimen of the tribe is exceptional.

3. A poem may be dangerous, but only to the poet or someone else of a creative mind.

4. Among critics there is an awareness of psychic heights and depths in the creative mind; it is thought that the finest poetry lies near these extremes. Gilbert Murray, for example, is sure that Sophocles was possessed by a series of devils when he wrote *Oedipus Rex*.

5. A prophecy can take place only after the presentation of a fact. Therefore prophetic (mystic or mantic) poetry is always reactive. Even though the prophecy is obscure it can be made intelligible to the waking mind. An utterance of the demon, on the other hand, is obscurity itself; we do not even know who or what said it.

6. Nothing can create the poem but toil. After the Delphian oracle had pronounced, the priestly assistant rendered the message into intelligible prose or verse.

All we can say about a poem like *Kubla Khan* is that it was given by the demon and versified by the poet, almost before he was awake. The assembling of references, traced by J. L. Lowes, tells the whole waking history of the poem. But there is a further secret. If Wordsworth had read everything Coleridge did and had fallen asleep over *Purchas His Pilgrimage*, he still would not have awakened to write *Kubla Khan*.

7. Poetry is but one form of expression of mystic or demonic vision. Religion, war, magic, the other fine arts are further forms.

8. Genius in art is probably only the intuitive knowledge of form.

9. The demonic poets are among the least prolific of artists and tend to despise the mob. The poets who love humanity often become mystics. Crane, however, thought his poems were for the people; this was part of the central delusion he picked up from Whitman. Elsewhere Crane asserted that he wanted to slap humanity in the face.

10. The struggle between Spender's mysticism and his socialism tends to result in the strengthening of the former. There is evidence in his manuscripts that he rejects material that "arrives." Above all, he is concerned with lucidity, Light as opposed to Obscurity. This is more than a poetic method; it is a direction of life.

11. By the process of elimination it might be shown that Williams is attracted to the depths of the poetic psyche, although the poem above indicates no such tendency. His most serious publications are charged with some force that arrives from a level below the calm. There is a sea-elephant in his poetry. But why he tries to still the waters is the question I cannot answer.

12. "The most typical and valid expression of the American *psychosis* seems to me still to be found in Whitman." One cannot believe that this was written by Crane unless he understands that by psychosis is meant nothing more than "the psychic process." But reading *psychosis* in the pathological sense, not intended by Crane, the statement gives us a truth.

13. Crane tried poison twice before he succeeded in killing himself by drowning. That he contemplated death is known, but we have no reason to believe that the sea exerted any morbid influence over the poet. The "evidence" in *Cape Hatteras* must be discarded.

14. To my knowledge, I have never seen a discarded poem that excelled the final form. On the other hand, no final poem can ever tell as much about the intention of the poet or about the poetic psyche as those worksheets which he almost systematically destroys.

Psychological Notes
on the Poetical Process

RUDOLF ARNHEIM

To Paolo Milano

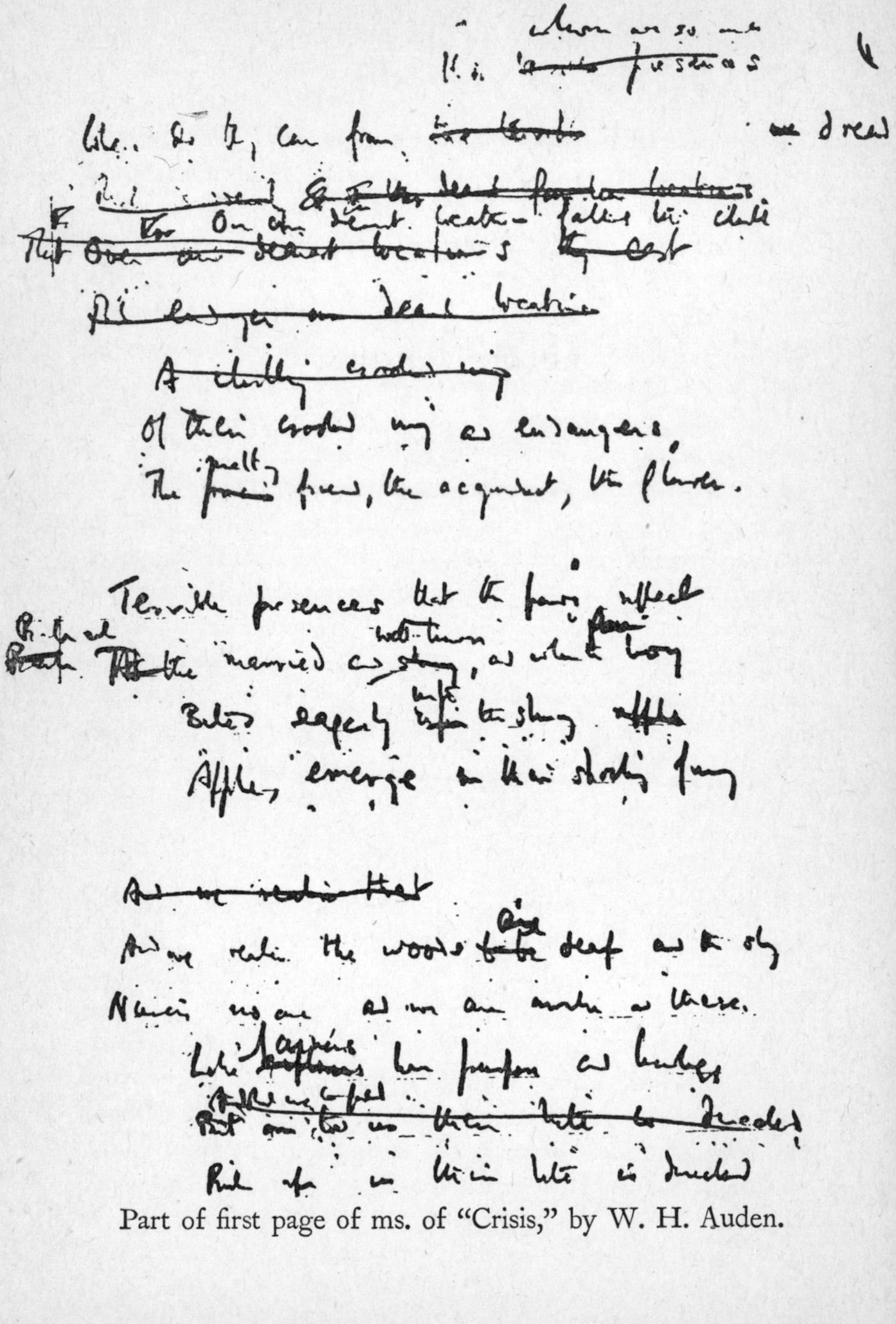

Part of first page of ms. of "Crisis," by W. H. Auden.

TIMES HAVE their tasks. Discoveries open new fields, restrictions exclude others; needs create curiosities. Thus it should not have been difficult to predict that sometime soon somebody with a flair for the cultural capacities and interests of Western man in our century would hit upon collecting the worksheets of poets. Not only as reliquiae, which allow the devout to address a tangible object; nor merely to provide evidence of the never quite believable existence of the master in the flesh; and not even mainly in order to help the understanding of the printed word by enabling the reader slowly to retrace the poet's trail from the plains to the heights, where breathing is heavy for the unacclimatized. Rather could it have been predicted that such a collection would be meant primarily for the study of the creative process, that curious end-product of a long phylogenetic development, during which the refinement of the organism's reactions to its environment has finally led, in man, to the capacity of producing interpretative images of what is exciting, puzzling, desirable.

I

The imprint of the creator. Concern with his own mind is an occupation characteristic of modern man. Only recently, interest in the psychological motives and rules of artistic activity has begun to complement and even to overshadow the traditional search for the norms of apt and beautiful representation. Until a few centuries ago, poets and other artists were essentially instruments for the picturing of the gods and the kings, the ideal of man, the struggle of the mortals for salvation. Many of the great buildings, statues, poems were anonymous, and when the artist or writer was praised it was because he succeeded in giving his subjects beauty, strength and truthfulness. One valued the things created while the act of creation was considered only in view of what it produced. The artists cleared their pictures and statues of the traces of handiwork. Michelangelo polished the marble until the surfaces displayed the perfection of what has grown from seed. Of course, many sculptors have kept on doing so until this very day. However, in the 19th century, it became possible for Rodin to include in the final form of a work what appears in Michelangelo only as a declaration of tragic failure: large remnants of the amorphous marble block otherwise transformed into human shape. Whether artistically successful or not, the conception here goes beyond the subject matter to comprise the creator's struggle with his medium as a part of what the spectator is meant to witness. Rodin also preserves the forceful imprints of finger and chisel, thus adding the visible effects of the sculptor's action to the forces expressed in the muscles of the figure. Similarly, the brush-strokes of a Velasquez, a Manet, a van Gogh, induce us to see the painting not as a purified substitute but as a man-made equivalent of its subject. In other words, the work of art presents itself not as an additional piece of nature but as an artefact, which frankly originates from a different sphere, and thus offers the exciting spectacle of man laboring to interpret God's word in his own language.

This emphasis on the "manual" element in artistic images is related to the psychological turn of modern thought, which strips experience of its objective character, revealing it as a creation of the mind. It is the offspring of an era in which dreams are not studied any more for what they might tell prophetically about events distant in space or time but are considered as belonging to a second reality, where the images, delivered from the command of the senses, appear, transform and combine at the service of the dreamer's insights, fears, desires. Similarly, novelists penetrate into the unexplored every-day world of the mind, where curious fragments of observation overstay their welcome and freely mingle with the past, where words act on each other like things, and flimsy gods and monstrous hybrids live a respected existence.

In this era of psychology, we have come to appreciate the human imprint even where it leads an almost clandestine existence. While I am writing I have in front of me a framed page from a 15th century Italian prayerbook. The carefully straightened rows of words are animated by a gentle internal movement. Every letter subtly deviates from the size and direction prescribed by the rule, but all of these small imperfections balance each other in an infallible rhythm. The stamp of organic vitality delightfully distinguishes the manuscript from print. Yet this result is unintentional. The craftsman's aim was objective precision. Hand and eye are harnessed to give clear, beautiful appearance to the Latin text. Colored initials and gold pay homage to the dignity of the prayer. One can see how any attempt to express *himself* in his calligraphic style or to give a personal interpretation of the text would have seemed sacrilegious to the monk, who effaced himself without question in the service of his task. Turning to the more recent past, one wonders what Beethoven would say if he knew that we reproduce his handwritten scores in facsimile. We admire the yellowed pages which are crowded with hardly decipherable strokes dashed on the paper by a passionately hurried hand. Violent cancellations tell of despair. Here is a man even more completely surrendered to his task. Are we permitted to make ourselves the uninvited witnesses of a struggling mind's birththroes or should we rather be content with the fair final copy of what the composer was striving for, what he meant to give?

Is there something inappropriate about man's increasing

interest in the mind and its manifestations? From where does it spring? Is it that people, bewildered by the affairs of the state, convinced that they can exercise no influence, or unwilling to have a share in the brutal battle of egoisms, withdraw to an inner world, where thought and passion seem unimpaired, where understanding seems possible and action not excluded? Or have psychiatrists induced us to hope that our unreasonable ways of living together can be improved if we overhaul the unknown but in all likelihood badly distorted mechanism which determines human behavior, that psychological knowledge and therapy may allow us efficiently to control the precious creative powers of the brain, which at present are as unruly as the weather? Or, finally, is our curiosity simply an extension of the interest in the forces of nature, which have always been the scientist's and artist's concern and which certainly include the dynamics of the mind?

II

Graphological aspects. It seemed pertinent to point to the psychological setting of our enterprise even though this is not the place for an attempt to answer the above questions. For our present purpose it suffices to acknowledge the spell which the manuscripts collected by the Lockwood Memorial Library exercise as soon as one opens their envelopes. They would fascinate the visitor even if they offered nothing else but the opportunity to see in the handwriting of the author the words familiar from neutral print. Whoever has preserved a feeling for visible expression is provided here with a check on his literary judgment. In one case, he may find his previous impression of genuine wealth confirmed by a true originality of form in the writing. In another case, an unexpected pedantic dryness or trivial extravagance may urge a more critical examination of a text that had seemed convincing. Or again, the simple strength of a handwriting may lead to the pleasant discovery of an author who had escaped his attention.

Indeed, the fact that many of the modern poets still master the dying-out craft of writing by hand suggests a number of possible psychological studies. Graphologists assert that the "quality" of a personality, i.e. the substantial richness which manifests itself in a man's looks, opinions, creations and the style of his life is also clearly observed in the handwriting, even though hard to define by measurable traits. The "form-niveau," as Ludwig Klages has called it, of the poets' hand-writings could be evaluated by experts. It could be determined to what extent the graphologists agree, and their judgment could be compared with the literary evaluation of critics. Again one could try to find out whether the handwritings of poets have common characteristics and whether differences can be related to the individual literary style. There is also the problem of the relationship between the person as he is known in life and the different person that may emerge from his work. A quick and admittedly unreliable check-up seems to suggest the possibility that the handwritings of the authors are more closely related to the physiognomy of their poems. If this supposition turned out to be correct one would be tempted to believe that in some cases artistic creation is not simply a direct expression of the spontaneous self or a tenuous, illusive façade but involves the creation of a new self, genuine enough to determine the handwriting. Controlled by value judgments, this "created" self would absorb the best resources of the person and, in turn, shape his artistic style.

Whatever the findings, it would appear that in the psychology of the poet, just as in the psychology of personality in general, graphology can be expected to fulfill a useful function. Handwriting seems to reflect rather directly and abstractly some of the basic dynamic factors—the "radix" or root, as Max Wertheimer used to call them—to which eventually the external symptoms of personality will have to be reduced. It presents them in visible patterns, which are more easily analyzed than the corresponding intangible forces of the mind.

Psychoanalysis and art. Other psychological investigations could take advantage of the important specialty of the Buffalo collection, which preserves poems in various successive versions and in this way allows insight into some of the stages of creative processes. During the last decades a narrow conception of what psychology is concerned with has been accepted to such an extent that the psychologist, whenever called upon, is almost automatically expected to supply a psychoanalytical interpretation of biographical "problems." This expectation seems symptomatic of a century in which so many people are more concerned with their troubles than with their tasks.

On the basis of what Freud and his followers have asserted about the function art fulfills in the household of the mind, we should be prepared to discover in the transformation from early to later versions of a poem developments of the following kind. At the first stages, the poem might be found to resemble the crude wishdreams by which man compensates himself for the disappointments of "real" life. Soon, however, the poet, aware of the fact that his customers would feel embarrassed to draw this kind of satisfaction from their reading as long as its purpose were stated nakedly, would proceed cleverly to disguise the true character of his work by subduing features which provided blunt wish-fulfillment. He would dim the description of happy triumph with a shade of discomfort, he would delay the climax of fulfillment, and "bribe"— as Freud puts it—the readers by covering the nudity of his vision with a respectable ballet skirt of "purely esthetic pleasure." Furthermore, whereas the primary conception, determined mainly by the manifestations of the unconscious, might resemble the mysterious chaos of a dream, later versions would show the effect of "secondary elaboration," by which the artist's ego would render the poem more coherent and comprehensible. Also one might have to expect that in the early drafts spontaneous self-expression would present sexual motives rather too crudely and that later in the process "symbols" would serve the function attributed to them by Freud, i.e. clothe the sinful with a transparent dress of innocence.

It is possible that a more confident investigator will discover such features. More probably will they be found neither to occur frequently nor to be capable of providing essential understanding of the process which creates good poems; and it is the good poems that deserve our main interest. Freud has admitted that he found confirmation of his esthetic theses not in "highly esteemed" writers but in "less pretentious" popular fiction. May we suggest that one of the reasons why these popular novels are bad is their conformity to the psychoanalytic theory of "sublimation"?

Undoubtedly, there is wish-fulfillment in many a work of art. But there are other motives. There is the urge to clarify and interpret the vagueness and disorder of the phenomenal world through artistic representation. There is the obsession with the painful, which Freud found so difficult to explain, the passion for cruelty and ugliness, the proclamation of life as a tragedy. Furthermore, not only the yearning for the beautiful but also, and perhaps more frequently, the enjoyment of it induces artistic expression. What is even more important, wish-fulfillment in true works of art should more properly be called presentation of the ideal; because its main characteristic is not that it expresses the subjectively desirable but that it attempts to realize nature's essence and aim. In the artistic process, the consideration of reality is far from being a secondary device for the concealing of crude wishdreams. The validity of an ideal depends on whether its primary conception does justice to essential objective aspects of its theme. Therefore we do not expect to find in the poetical process a development from spontaneous wish-dreaming to a secondary approximation of reality.

Furthermore we cannot accept Freud's outmoded l'art-pour-l'art idea of artistic form. Form is not a sugar-coating of sensory pleasure secondarily applied to a statement of facts or fancies. Form is the very essence of artistic representation. It therefore cannot be expected to make its entry at an advanced stage of the poetical process.

Nor is there any evidence that unconscious impulses, in the Freudian sense of the term, prevail in the first formation of the work of art. While it seems to be true that the artist remains unaware of many early processes, they are unlikely to be essentially instinctive. The whole range of the mental capacities which participate in the conscious elaboration of the work, such as observing, feeling, thinking, organizing, can be assumed to function under cover already in the mysterious first stages of artistic conception. In particular, it seems difficult to believe that the early impulses should be mainly sexual. The limitation of an artist who shared the monomania of an oversexed civilization would hardly qualify him to create a valid image of reality.

Thus I do not anticipate that Freudian esthetics will be of help in the interpretation of our worksheets. The trouble with the psychoanalysis of art in its present state is that it seems suitable only for the understanding of some secondary features and common adulterations of the artistic process.

Projective techniques. Psychoanalysis is probably an early phase of a much broader psychological approach, which will compensate in due time for a kind of esthetic theory too exclusively concerned with the relationship of the work of art to external reality. An indivisible unity of the inner and the outer world constitutes man's "lebensraum," with the one constantly shaping the other. Psychology is likely to develop toward such a conception. It will enlarge the range of the conative factors acknowledged by the Freudians. It will realize that there are powerful personal constants which are not essentially conative. And it will search for the proper equilibration of the subjective and the objective.

This is of particular importance for the understanding of the work of art, which is not concerned with the objective nature of things alone—as any scientific statement is—but includes in its image of the universe the "personal equation" of the creator. From the viewpoint of science, any artistic representation, for instance Flaubert's or Stendhal's conception of man, is one-sided. However, esthetically it can be complete and valid. In science, the personal approach of any one investigator or school of thought represents a limitation to be overcome in the interest of objective truth; whereas, in the field of art, Flaubert's pessimistic realism and Stendhal's noble "espagnolisme" are just as much a part of the truth as the objective traits of the society which they both portray.

Psychologists are using the so-called "projective techniques" in order to study the influence of personality factors on man's dealing with his environment. For this research art offers a promising but so far almost untouched material. There is no more sensitive instrument for the recording of the central mental activities. With regard to subject matter, we expect the artist to select topics which he happens to know and which interest him; to avoid others which leave him indifferent. He may also be the kind of person who keeps away from what is frightening, puzzling, unpleasant. Depending on his temperament, he may be inclined to see conflict rather than harmony, to present dynamic action or else static configuration. Paul Valéry acknowledges the "return of terms which reveal the tendencies, the frequent characteristics of a mind. (Certain words resound in us among all others like harmonics of our profoundest nature.)" In the same way, there is affinity with specific colors, spatial directions, musical forms, poetical rhythms. Simplicity may be preferred to complexity, idealized beauty to realism; or vice versa. Caroline F. E. Spurgeon tells us that Shakespeare's metaphors reveal a predominant interest in movement and the change and contrast of color and that "if we except the human body, images from birds form by far the largest section drawn from any class of objects." This cannot but remind the psychologist of the Rorschach test, a projective technique which is based on the hypothesis that specific emotional and intellectual personality aspects account for the elements of movement, color, subject matter, etc., in people's responses to inkblots. The discovery of such meeting-places augurs well for a future co-ordination of literary and psychological research.

The scientific analysis of projective factors will further our insight into the nature and causes of "style." Psychological findings will be welcomed by the art historians and literary critics, who are trying to get beyond the mere description of the various forms produced by different cultural periods and individual artists.

However, psychologists will have to be wary of a tendency which is clearly expressed in the term "projective." They must realize that a human being's account and fashioning of his environment is not simply the projection of a subjective pattern on amorphous experience material. The difference between the Rorschach inkblots and the world to which man responds is that life situations commonly possess a more clean-cut structure in themselves. To the artistic product applies what we asserted before about man's life-activity in general: it springs from an interplay of the given object-structure on the one hand and the artist's "temperament" on the other.

Subjective vision is esthetically valid only if it does justice to essential aspects of its "reference," as the semanticists call it.

Valuable insight into the projective factors of poetical creation may come from the study of worksheets. Even though there is no such thing as the absolute priority of either the subjective or the objective element, one may try to find out, for example, whether the personal factors are particularly strong in early drafts and tend to be complemented later in the interest of a more universally valid representation; or whether, on the contrary, they emerge more clearly in the course of elaboration. Great individual differences are likely to obtain and may uncover relevant style characteristics. Unfortunately, no examples of such analysis can be given in this exploratory study because projective factors can be determined only through the comparative investigation of a large number of cases.

The psychology of adequate representation. The approaches reviewed so far promise to increase our knowledge of the influence which the personality of the artist exercises on his work. However, the psychologist may hope to be equally useful in elucidating the role which the given data of objective reality play in artistic representation. He can try to obtain evidence of the laborious process by which the poet strives for the adequate rendering of an experience. Little is known about the early stages of artistic conception. Hypotheses on their nature are largely deduced from the psychological and esthetic principles to which the investigator subscribes. He may expect, for instance, that early drafts will contain rather literal and complete transcriptions of the original experience while later ones will show attempts to sift and transform these in the direction of greater beauty or deeper significance. If his ideas about the psychology of thought and language are different he may anticipate, on the contrary, that the formative process will constitute a gradual approximation to the specific original experience.

In either case the investigator will consider the successive transformations of the poetical text as determined by the requirements of the task of representation itself. This approach is nearest to the spirit of gestalt psychology. In their early investigations of visual perception, the gestaltists have shown that what we see when viewing a pattern is derived not simply from past experiences, preferences, or expectations but, to a great extent, from the structure of the given configuration. In the field of thinking, it has been demonstrated that the obstacles which hamper the solution of a task are often inherent in the problem situation, which suggests connections, segregations and emphases unsuitable to immediate insight. Similarly, the gestaltists have pointed out that in social life selfish and egotistic tendencies of the individual are counteracted by a capacity to evaluate objectively the demands of a group situation. This led finally to a theory of ethics which emphasizes the derivation of values from objective conditions rather than from traditional norms. It is this stress of objective requirements as a motive of human action which suggests that a psychology of art based on gestalt principles will be particularly rewarding.

Thus when we sift the shavings which have fallen from the work-bench of the poet we expect to find indications of a lawful development in the direction of appropriate, precise, unified form. The evidence will be far from complete because only a few of the actual stages precipitate in writing. Nor can we expect one straight trail to lead from the first attempt to the final version. Experiences in the psychology of thinking suggest that there will be dead-ends, new starts, moments of almost blind searching, and many instances of a dramatic "restructuring" of the whole. However, the analysis of any sub-whole of the process as well as of its over-all course is likely to show consistent growth, a striving constantly controlled by the vision of a temporary or final aim, a complex totality in which every step has its logical function.

The outcome of such an analysis is curiously dependent on the artistic quality of the material. Offhand, one might think it would not make much difference to the psychologist whether he was dealing with a good or a bad writer. However, I have already suggested that a particular kind of motive will be found to be responsible for certain types of bad literature. In general, an informal examination of some of the Buffalo material made me wonder whether the process of lawful development toward the final aim might not be found more clearly in the better poets. As the quality decreases, the changes from stage to stage would appear to be more accidental, i.e. caused by momentary impulses, the last version putting an end rather arbitrarily to an inherently endless succession of transformations. If this supposition turned out to be correct, the inner necessity of the sequence of steps which leads to the final form would be one criterion of artistic quality—a finding that would agree with what is known about the psychology of successful thinking.

III

The abstractness of language. In the second section of this paper I have surveyed psychological methods which can be applied to the study of the poetical process. I propose to devote the third to a more detailed discussion of some of the factors that play a role in "representation," i.e. the mental activity which provides adequate literary form for poetical experiences. In this exploratory study it will not be possible to substantiate propositions with sufficient evidence. I cannot hope to give more than a few suggestions for future research. At some points, examples will show that the worksheets of poets provide insight which could not be gained from other sources.

Artistic representation is frequently considered to be a direct, "cosmetic" transformation of the raw material of experience. The poet is said merely to omit or add elements, to change or distort, dissociate or reassemble what he has observed. Such a view neglects the basic distinction between an experience and its representation in an artistic medium. The original vision of, say, the glassy surface-quality of a waterfall may be quite precise as to its perceptual, expressive, and emotional characteristics. However, such an experience is not manifest primarily either in lines or colors which could simply be transferred to canvas nor in words which could be recorded on paper. Henri Bergson, in his *Introduction to Metaphysics*, has pointed out that there are two profoundly different ways of grasping a thing: we either turn about it or enter into it. The latter method refers to the direct, "intuitive" vision of the nature of the object, whereas the former indicates the often long and laborious task of fitting the experience to suitable means of representation provided by a particular medium, such as the concepts of scientific or literary language. There is no direct transformation of experience into form but rather a search for equivalents.

The specific characteristics of various artistic media account for the different effects which can be obtained through them. The painter may represent a cemetery by offering an image of its visual appearance. In doing so, he cannot but emphasize specific expressive qualities of the subject, such as its sadness or the peace of the resting-place. The composer Saint-Saëns, in his Danse Macabre, imitates some specific acoustical traits, such as the rattle of the bones or the cry of the cock. Apart from these pictorial elements, he renders the morbid rapture of the death-dance through "abstract" sound and rhythm in a way which specifies the expression and feeling-tone of his experience. He does not identify the churchyard, as the painter necessarily would (unless he used "non-objective" form). The composer portrays no specific thing. At the most, he permits reference to a range of possible physical or psychological situations which his musical structure would fit. When the poet says "cemetery," he identifies a species of physical place by a group-name, but specifies neither the perceptual nor the expressive attributes of graveyards. "Darkness" designates a perceptual quality, "fear" an emotion. None of these three words, while likely to evoke the kind of content specified by the other two, identifies it in particular. That is, cemetery may be associated with fear but also with serenity; darkness, with a cemetery or a movie theater; fear, with darkness or glaring light. Words, the building stones of language, either designate general attributes without indicating the objects to which these belong or identify individuals or groups of things without specifying their attributes.

The emptiness of concepts permits statements that imply no other characteristics than the few on which the speaker and the listener are agreed. To be able to tell of "a man who showed me to the station" without having to communicate the details of his appearance is helpful in keeping the information to its essentials. If I need to specify I can do so by using a different term ("bootblack") or by adding one ("an elderly man"). Thus language fits an important trait of human thinking and behaving: we tend not to specify and differentiate beyond the degree required by the situation. Or, in other words, we keep our concepts, intentions, etc., as abstract as the circumstances permit.

Different needs and interests lead to linguistic differentiation in varying areas. The Eskimos have different words for "snow on the ground," "falling snow," "drifting snow," "a snowdrift" (Franz Boas). An automobile-addict carefully distinguishes Fords, Cadillacs, Chryslers, whereas for his neighbor a car may be just one kind of thing for which he does not need more than one word. Primitive languages connect by a common prefix the names of objects which have a common perceptual trait, e.g. all round things: circular movements, clouds, stars, hills, fruits, stones, round hats, crowds of animals or people; for us, this common property is of no practical importance. Again, a primitive language may possess a score of particular words indicating different varieties of gait—one walks leaning forward, or backward; swaying from side to side; slouchingly or smartly; swaggeringly; swinging one's arms, or only one arm; head down or up, or otherwise (L. Lévy-Bruhl). Western man does not possess the corresponding specific terms or when he does he uses them rarely because, under the influence of modern natural science, the "physiognomic" qualities of shape, movement, etc., have lost their vital importance for effective dealing with the problems of daily life. For our practical purposes, the significance of a man's walking is largely limited to the mere abstract change of place.

Poetical concreteness. The increasing detachment of modern language from the perceptual appearance of things poses a problem for the poet. It is true that the law of parsimony holds even more severely for poetry than for the loose speech of the streets: specification must not go beyond the requirement. However, the poet's task consists not simply in the identification of things and events. He has to convey the vivid experience of the forces which make a phenomenon expressive. These forces are active essentially through the senses. Somebody may tell us correctly but quite unpoetically that the eternal repetition of the seawater's movement suggests a conception of time very different from the one which emerges from the daily strivings of man. T. S. Eliot, in the third of his *Four Quartets*, gives artistic reality to this thought by capturing the movement of the sea in the perceptually effective beat of the bell and by embodying the dynamics of human striving in the image of worrying women.

> The tolling bell
> Measures time not our time, rung by the unhurried
> Ground swell, a time
> Older than the time of chronometers, older
> Than time counted by anxious worried women
> Lying awake, calculating the future,
> Trying to unweave, unwind, unravel . . .

The ways of "practical" language seem to influence early versions of poems. The poet's primary experience may well contain a precise feeling of the perceptual qualities which carry the crucial expression. Yet as he searches for an equivalent in the medium of words he will often be inclined at first to use the most abstract practical name, which may call to mind things but not actually convey their characteristics charged with expression. Thus, the following early draft of a passage in Keats' "Hyperion" (I, 7-9):

> No stir of air was there,
> Not so much life as on a summer's day
> Robs not at all the dandelion's fleece

leads to this final version:

> No stir of air was there,
> Not so much life as on a summer's day
> Robs not one light seed from the feather'd grass.

The precision of the botanist suggested by practical language ("dandelion") is given up in favor of a description which omits the identification of the plant but specifies the expressive perceptual features of weight and movement.

Practical language also tends to state the meaning and cause of a phenomenon rather than its mere appearance because these interpretative factors are valuable for orientation and reaction in life. In a letter dated February 14, 1819, Keats drafts the third stanza of "La Belle Dame Sans Merci" as follows:

> I see death's lilly on thy brow
> With anguish moist and fever dew
> And on thy cheeks death's fading rose
> Withereth too.

This is immediately changed into:

> I see a lilly on thy brow
> With anguish moist and fever dew
> And on thy cheeks a fading rose
> Fast withereth too.

That is, in the final form the poet omits the diagnosis ("death") but keeps the symptoms. The mere uninterpreted description of the pale face provides the shock of discovery. The draft-version tended to reduce the visible signs to mere factual attributes of death. After the correction, paleness strikes the inner eye as the physical effect of a concrete, though unnamed power.

The transfiguration of the concrete. If it be true that the poet frequently renders an experience by stressing the perceptual features which make it expressive, one may wonder whether such a recourse to concreteness does not interfere with another important task of poetry. As I said before, one of the virtues of language is its abstractness, by which it can limit the description of an event to the essentials, to what is generally valid. In naming an object or happening, language assigns the individual case to a group and by such classification helps man to orient himself in the environment. All art, including poetry, is supposed to serve the similar function of revealing the general nature of things rather than recording their individual manifestations. If so, is this useful function of art not jeopardized when in the course of the formative process the poet presses for the representation of specific characteristics?

This objection would seem to be based on a misunderstanding. Perceptual concreteness does not exclude abstraction in the sense of an emphasis of essentials. The poet does not cite concrete details indiscriminately but stresses the features which made the subject artistically pregnant for him. The peculiar ringing of an inner alarm-bell which indicates to the artist that a particular thing or happening is usable material seems to be related to the conscious or unconscious feeling that the subject presents or at least suggests a clear-cut, concentrated image of a significant life-situation. Modern man has become capable of thinking in theoretical concepts, but he is still in constant search of perceptual "models," which will allow him to deal with universals in the tangible form of concrete application. Any work of art offers just such a model situation. It stresses and clarifies features which symbolize the general significance of its specific subject matter. Hence the incorporeal transparency which, for all its vigorous concreteness, distinguishes the masterpiece from the vulgar, material heaviness of a minor work. The latter does not sufficiently transcend the particular case it presents. The masterwork embraces the whole range of human experience from the sensory perceptions to rarefied ideas. In fact, it often expresses the most abstract meaning through the most elementary stimulation. An example from painting may illustrate this point. In Delacroix' later pictures the color scheme is reduced to a violent conflict of pure red and deep green. In this way, the appearance of concrete objects—fluttering coats of Arabian horseback riders, bleeding tigers, the impenetrable woods and the agitated waves of the ocean—is visibly referred back to the dramatic counterpoint of fiery passion versus the cool succulence of organic substance, i.e. to the deep meaning which the painter saw embodied in his romantic subjects. By abstracting natural appearance in the direction of basic expressive values the artist evokes the universal in the specific.

This transfiguration of the concrete can be observed in the poetical process. The Buffalo collection possesses the draft of an unpublished poem by Aldous Huxley "about driving a car at night and the symbolic significance of the narrow universe created by the headlights." In the poem, the traces of the scene which, according to the author's comment, inspired it are largely effaced.

> In the chaos of the moon's
> Absence one creative beam
> Shapes the narrow world through which we fly. . . .

Of a complex natural situation nothing is kept but the factors which suggest symbolic meaning: the confused darkness in which a searching light discovers comprehensible bits. The adjective "creative" lifts the event expressly to the spiritual level.

The degree to which, in a work of art, the physical situation is dematerialized represents a style factor, which varies with the author's attitude to reality and that of his period. But in any style the adequate dosage of reality-substance on the one hand and abstracted meaningful features on the other would seem to be one of the secrets of artistic achievement. Marks of the struggle for the right proportion are likely to be found in the worksheets of poets. It is a struggle particularly significant for the art of a period in which the attitude to reality represents a crucial problem.

The practical and the poetical. Aldous Huxley's poem offers also an example of another characteristic difference between practical every-day language and poetical expression. He speaks of animals discovered in the dark by the headlights. The first version reads:

> Calling up the momentary gleam

but the "momentary" is immediately substituted and transferred to the next line:

> Calling up the startled gleam
> Of momentary eyes and passing wing.

This leads to:

> Calling into life the gleam
> Of momentary wing and startled eye.

And finally:

> Calling up from nothingness
> Startled wing and momentary eye.

Probably, several factors are responsible for the changes which I am quoting in a somewhat simplified form. One of these factors is particularly interesting for our discussion, namely the quick shift from objective correctness, which is valuable for practical orientation, to a subjective truth, which may be decisive for the poetical experience. Objectively, there are animals whose existence is momentarily revealed by the beam of light. Subjectively, however, these animals exist only for the short moment during which they are seen. An observer who uses his eyes for the purpose of practical orientation will immediately deduce the objective situation from the subjective sight by means of his past experience. But for the poet the dependence of existence on observation is exactly what attracted his attention because it symbolizes an aspect of man's attitude to reality. Therefore the changes from the objectively correct "momentary gleam" to the objectively wrong but subjectively accurate "momentary eyes." Something similar occurs for the expression of alarm, which belongs objectively most directly to the eyes of the animals stirred by the light, but is subjectively enhanced by the suddenness of the reflection. Hence the objectively incorrect but poetically fitting "startled gleam." The "startled eye" in the following version represents a regression to the more practical, objective language. (This is an example of the fluctuations which occur in the striving for final expression.) Huxley ends up with "startled wing and momentary eye"—a double deviation from the practically reasonable, designed to intensify the experience which the reader is invited to share.

Another illustration of the shift from the practically correct to the poetically relevant is found in one of Stephen Spender's worksheets. Again we can observe how the writer is induced at first by practical thought and language to use a formulation which he has to revise in order to do better justice to his subject. A first version:

> What is the use now of meeting and speaking:
> Always when we meet I think of another meeting
> Always when we speak I think of another speaking

is transformed into:

> Oh what is the use now of our meeting and speaking
> Since every meeting is thinking of another meeting
> Since all my speaking is groping for another speaking.

Although the first version makes the situation quite clear, it stresses, in the syntactic structure of its second and third lines, practically relevant aspects instead of the poetically crucial ones. The reader's attention is focused on the mere coincidence in time of two kinds of happenings: the physical meeting and speaking on the one hand, the psychological thinking on the other. Similarly, in the first version, the grammatical subjects of the two sentences emphasize the persons involved: when *we* do this, *I* do that. But the practical information about time relationships and the "cast" seems not to have been essential poetically. The poet finds the decisive issue in a paradox, namely the identity of two contradictory happenings: physical contact and psychological aloofness. By reformulating his description in a fashion which is strange to practical usage the poet achieves a closer correspondence of form and meaning. He transforms the time relationship into an equation

meeting = thinking of another meeting
speaking = groping for another speaking

and by suppressing the original subjects (we and I) he subordinates the protagonists of the practical scene to those of the poetically relevant happening, namely the meeting and the thinking, the speaking and the groping, which are now fittingly equated.

Thus, the analysis of poetical manipulation suggests again that linguistic form is not obtained directly from the primary experience but must be considered a re-creation within the medium, subject to the particularities of the medium.* The effects on language of the function which it serves in daily life constitute a particularity of the literary medium. Analogous tendencies to go beyond "practically" important characteristics of things can be observed in the visual arts.

The search for the specific. The indefiniteness of words, to which I referred before, suggests that the literary recording

* The examples may also serve as modest illustrations of the fact that "poetic" language is not distinguished from the practical by expressing in a deliberately unusual, ornamental manner what we say straight in everyday life, but rather by offering equally straight, adequate formulations of subjects which differ from those with which practical speech is typically concerned. The difference of form springs from a difference of content.

of an experience resembles, in its first stages, the trapping of an insect with a large net. The little animal is being confined to a limited area but not yet pinned to a specific spot. The worksheets show how the poet closes in gradually on the adequate formulation. As an example I will quote from Stephen Spender's drafts of a poem ("Abrupt and charming mover"), one of which is partially given below. The first line, "Like a skater," read in an earlier version "Like dancers." The cold charm of the girl's personality may have seemed fittingly translated into the visible by dance performances of the ballet-type. But at the time the poet made the change he may have realized that the concept "dancer," in addition to covering the light entertainment he had in mind, could also refer to the deeply felt compositions of a "modern" dancer—the very opposite of what he was trying to convey. The example shows that whereas logically a concept may possess a constant sum of attributes, psychologically its content varies because the context in which it appears sheds light on some of its aspects while temporarily blacking out others. Max Wertheimer, in his investigation of the syllogism, has shown that productive conclusions are often due to the capacity of the thinker to use his concepts beyond the limitations imposed on them by the primary context. Similarly, a writer, confined at first to the specific meaning that suggested the use of a given term, has then to free himself of this limitation in order to examine the additional or different meanings which the term may also convey. Failure to consider the "objective" range of words accounts for much unsuccessful writing in poetry and prose.

"Skater" is better than "dancer" because the pirouettes on ice illustrate exactly the lack of emotional involvement for which the poet needed an image. The concept "dancer" turns out to be too large with regard to the pertinent attribute. "Skater" is unambiguous in this respect and therefore renders the comparison with the woman more precise.

A little later in the same draft Mr. Spender wishes to say that the woman, like the skater, somehow attracts the heart but never "can touch beneath the senses' glassy surface." The worksheet reveals how he experimented with various verbs in order to identify the specific kind of effect on the "heart." He tries "tempting," "binding," "drawing," then decides for "enchants the heart." An analysis would show that each of the first three words contains the element of attraction but either leaves out the specific connotation desired or adds unsuitable ones; while "enchants" aptly describes the effect created by a mere spell.

Thus the primary experience is often matched at first with concepts which belong to the general area of the meaning to be conveyed. These concepts overlap the meaning but do not "pinpoint" it. Which brings us back to our earlier assertion that representation does not consist in the mere selection and combination of reality-elements but rather in the construction of a fitting pattern drawn from a system of pre-existing forms. An experience meets an artistic medium, which possesses specific capacities of expression. The two have to put up with each other as best they can.

Physiognomic qualities. One of the means by which the poet gives concrete expression to ideas or to physical or psychological phenomena is related to what has been said earlier about primitive language. The poet is accustomed to rely on perceptual kinships of a kind which until recently had no place in our scientific conception of the world and which are rarely expressed in our practical language. It is true that we speak without hesitation of a "soft tune" thus applying a quality of touch to sounds, or of a "cold color," which relates temperature to an optical phenomenon. However, we do so not because we consciously acknowledge that there are qualitative similarities between perceptions derived from different senses, but rather because words like "cold," "sharp," "high," "dark" have partially lost their specific perceptual connotation for us and are now used to designate more general expressive values. However, this linguistic phenomenon itself bears witness to the fact that it is natural for man to rely on qualities which different senses have in common. These similarities are fundamental for the primitives' conception of physical relationships. They provide the bases of metaphoric speech in poetry. I quote one of the versions of the Spender passage we have been considering:

> Like a skater
> Who with sweeping silk
> Enchants the heart, but never never
> Can touch beneath the senses' glassy surface,
> So you daily weave
> Over all that's impenetrable, delight.
> For me there's no
> Fulfilment of the ripened luminary,
> Only attraction of the snow.

Silk, glassy, luminary, snow. Later versions contain in addition: "There is no warmth, no kinship" and "No sanguine calm to rest the eyes" or "No mild and sanguine image." Thus the poet experiments with various perceptual attributes of touch, vision, temperature, and motion in order to express the psychology of the woman.

The scientific explanation of this linguistic usage is still in its earliest stages. Gestalt psychologists have emphasized it as an example of "isomorphism," i.e. of structural similarity among phenomena which pertain to different physical or psychological media. The psychological kinship of, say, red wine, velvet, and the sound of a violoncello would be explainable if the physiological stimuli which correspond to these experiences produced effects on the nervous system that resembled each other structurally. Von Hornbostel has pointed out in this connection that in simple organisms there is a close unity of various sensory areas, which become differentiated only in more advanced phases of evolution. He states that what the senses have in common is more important than their differences. This means that "physiognomic" or expressive qualities which are largely independent of the particular medium in which they appear are probably much more basic in perceptual experience than those which psychologists were accustomed to consider as primary: hue, brightness, pitch, size, shape, etc. The poet, then, in freely connecting phenomena from various areas of experience relies on a fundamental trait of human perception.

It may be said in passing that the term "pathetic fallacy" implies a painful misunderstanding based on a conception of the world which stresses material differences and neglects structural analogies. When Torquato Tasso relates the wailing of the wind and the dewdrops shed by the stars to the departure of his love he is not pretending to believe in a fallacious animism, which endows nature with sympathetic feeling, but is using genuine structural similarities of the perceivable behavior of wind and water on the one hand and the experience and expression of grief on the other.

The role of imagination. Schopenhauer, in *Die Welt als Wille und Vorstellung,* praises the abstractness of words for the reason that it permits the reader through his imagination to supply the missing concrete detail in accordance with his individuality, sphere of knowledge, and personal whim. The opportunity of filling the framework of the literary text with private furniture is supposed to account for the fact that "literature exercises a stronger, deeper, more universal effect than pictures or statues." Schopenhauer defines literature as "the art of calling the imagination into play by means of words."

This view tacitly implies the validity of the traditional psychological theory according to which the mind cannot picture anything but fully concrete, individual images. If this theory were correct, then, in fact, the abstractness of the contents conveyed through language would require the reader's or listener's imagination to supply the missing details.

However, esthetic considerations suggest that to enlist the services of imagination for the appreciation of art is dangerous. It encourages the attitude of the concertgoer who uses the musical sound as a mere starting point from which to float on the stream of consciousness through fanciful landscapes. It justifies the behavior of people whom a Dutch scene in painting induces to dream back to the sights of their honeymoon trip to Europe. None of us is free of such fancies, but we must realize that they distract our attention from the appreciation of works of art rather than enhance our understanding. This is also true for literature, even though words gain meaning only through the past experience of the reader. In practice, the reactions of readers vary widely in this respect. There are those who visualize the persons and places of a novel with photographic exactness. Others have no imagery at all. They do hardly more than acknowledge the meaning of the words, yet may be vividly touched by the expressive values of the text. The reader who uses the literary text as a mere skeleton which he has to enliven with his own flesh and blood is likely to distort the author's conception. Ample supplementary activity of the imagination is innocuous only (a) if it further develops the content of the text along structural lines set down by the author, (b) if it does not go beyond the highest degree of concreteness compatible with the style of the particular writing.

The latter point is of importance for our further discussion. Recent psychological studies have shown that imagination, far from portraying everything with the automatic faithfulness of the camera, may dwell on any level of abstraction. Similarly, literary styles are known to vary widely in this respect. The realistic novelist has his motif carried by hundreds of details as though they were so many reflecting facets. The happenings which he recounts impart their specific significance only if they are felt to be materially existent. On the other hand, the scarcity of specific characterization in a Boccaccio story or in Voltaire's *Candide* makes for a more rarefied literary climate, in which the characters are to be taken as mere types of human attitude. Their adventures, which might have been distasteful or absurd if the shadows had drunk of the blood of life, appear as playfully overdone. They are mere symbolizations of human aspiration and failure. Obviously, if a reader by means of his imagination endows all the violations of Cunégonde's womanhood with the concreteness of the pain felt by the cat which, in Flaubert's *Bouvard et Pécuchet*, escapes from a kettle of boiling water, he destroys the very substance of the author's conception. Conversely, Flaubert's cat serves its function only if its suffering is experienced as cruelly real.

Metaphor and simile. The search for the adequate level of abstractness is likely to play a role in the poetical process and to be demonstrable in literary worksheets. In this connection, a psychological analysis of the transformations which occur when the poet handles metaphors and similes is particularly promising. The following remarks suggest a theoretical basis for such investigations.

What is the poetical function of metaphors? A glance at recent studies on the subject shows that metaphors are no longer considered mere flourishes designed to make literary statements more colorful and to demonstrate the writer's virtuosity in the discovery of "the similar in the dissimilar." John Middleton Murry describes the metaphor as "the means by which the less familiar is assimilated to the more familiar, the unknown to the known." This use of comparisons would seem to be more didactic than poetic. We find it in scientific exposition, e.g. when atomic structure is described by a reference to the solar system. More frequently the simile serves to elucidate the essentials of a situation through the example of another one which is not necessarily better known but more concrete than the original. Thus, Stephen Spender describes the relatively intangible character of a human personality by speaking of a skater, of sweeping silk, of glassy surface. Even so, metaphors and similes are not essentially explanatory devices. When, in *Henry V,* it is said of the contending kingdoms of France and England that "their very shores look pale with envy of each other's happiness," the purpose is not to describe the looks of the chalky coasts by a reference to the more familiar paleness of faces; or vice versa. Is this metaphor useless to a reader who, from first-hand experience, knows the Channel coasts and also the paleness of jealous faces? On the contrary, he will find it more powerful.

Later in his essay, Murry calls the poetical metaphor "chiefly a means to excite in us a vague and heightened awareness of qualities we can best call spiritual" and "the analogy by which the human mind explores the universe of quality and charts the non-measurable world." Can the psychology of language account for this effect of the literary device?

A metaphor connects two or more segments of reality, such as the Channel coasts and the pale face. Exactly in what way do these segments co-exist in the mind of the reader or listener? Stephen J. Brown asserts that the image is momentarily substituted for the thing or happening it interprets. However, if, in the reader's mind, a pale face eclipsed the cliffs of Dover and Calais, the creative merger of the two components would obviously not occur. Brown's contention seems to be based on the above-cited psychological assumption that mental images are possible only in full concreteness; hence more than one of them could not occupy consciousness at the same time. If, however, we remember that mental images admit various levels of abstractness and that psychologically the content of a concept depends on the context in which it appears, another explanation suggests itself. When heterogeneous segments of reality are forced into one grammatical whole a structural conflict results, which must be resolved. Structural unity can be obtained on the basis of certain physiognomic qualities which the components have in common. Therefore, the discordant aspects of the components will retreat, the common ones will come to the fore. Naturally, by this I do not mean that nothing but the quality of paleness will remain of Shakespeare's above-quoted metaphor. Little would be gained by that. Rather do I suggest that, negatively, the reality-character of the components becomes subdued and that, positively, the physiognomic qualities common to the components are vigorously underscored in each. Thus, by their combination the components are driven to become more abstract; but the abstracted qualities continue to draw life blood from the reality contexts in which they are presented—subdued as these contexts may be.

In the whole-structure created by a metaphor, components which are and remain separate on the reality level unite on the level of physiognomic qualities. The metaphor, then, distills from reality-situations the deeper, underlying aspects of life, for whose sake alone art creates images of reality. This, I believe, is the metaphor's capacity of evoking the "spiritual," of "exploring the universe of quality."

Degrees of metaphoric abstraction. The looser the connection between components, the smaller will be the degree of the resulting abstraction. For instance, in the similes which Dante uses in the *Divina Commedia* an aspect of the story is compared to another situation, which is presented in a small, detailed, self-contained tale tied to the main story by nothing but a conjunction.

As sheep come forth from the pen, in ones, in twos, in threes, and the others stand all timid, casting eye and nose to earth, and what the first one doeth, the others do also, huddling up to her if she stand still, silly and quiet, and know not why, so saw I then the head of that happy flock move to come on, modest in countenance, in movement dignified. (*Purg*. III, 79-87, trans. Thomas Okey.)

The simile vivifies a particular physiognomic quality, but forces little abstraction on the two components. They remain relatively isolated and can therefore retain the realism cherished in the century of Giotto. When, on the other hand, the grammatical construction merges the segments of reality into a strongly unified whole these segments must lose concreteness. Otherwise, the construction would either split up into incompatible elements or give birth, on the reality level, to a surrealist monster. To test this thesis the reader has only to experiment for a moment with such metaphors as Romeo being stabbed with a white wench's black eye or heaven stopping the nose at the crime laid to Desdemona.

The modern metaphor. The comparison provided by the metaphor not only emphasizes certain physiognomic qualities in the primary situation, but also imbues it with the flavor of the second situation. That is, by introducing the word "stabbing" Shakespeare not only stresses the aggressiveness which stabbing and the white wench's black eye have in common but also imports into the love situation the atmosphere of murder.* In this particular instance the connotation of the metaphor obviously exaggerates the ferocity of the attack on Romeo, thus creating a subtly humorous effect. Probably the relations between the "universes" which are joined in the metaphor by the bridge of their common qualities are a revealing characteristic of an author's literary style. One has only to compare Homer's rose-fingered dawn with Eliot's metaphoric fusion of the divebomber and the dove of the Holy Ghost ("The dove descending breaks the air With flame of incandescent terror," *Four Quartets*) in order to realize that in the first case the two components, the morning sky and the young goddess, are concordant in atmosphere whereas in the modern example the common element of the bird forces the violent contrast of supreme love and supreme murder into a tightly integrated whole. Employed this way, the metaphor becomes a means of expressing comic or tragic or tragicomic contradiction and conflict. (Bad metaphors often unintentionally produce a humorous effect.)

Incompatibility of the components, in addition to making the metaphor one of the devices by which modern art repre-

* The metaphors produced in dreams have been interpreted by Freud as disguised presentations of objectionable contents. This theory seems limited, because dream symbolism is so universal; it applies to so many cases in which no plausible reason for camouflage can be discovered even if one admits that the unconscious censor may be much more prudish than the conscious ego. One might speculate therefore whether, in dreams, imagination does not regress to the primitive perceptual world, to that "universe wherein quality leaps to cohere with quality across the abysms of classification that divide and category the universe of intellectual apprehension" (J. M. Murry). The symbolic analogies which are made possible by this evocation of primordial affinities might often serve the purpose which, as I have just described, they do in poetry, namely they may imbue the primary object with suitable connotations. Thus, if in a dream a house substitutes for a woman, this may, in some cases, occur as a disguised allusion to the woman's receptive sexual role but it may also associate her with the qualities of hominess, security, protection, comfort, etc.

sents the contradictions of our life, serves also to increase abstractness. This is in keeping with another trait of modern art, namely its trend toward the dematerialization of reality. For the same purpose, the modern metaphor tends to eliminate the difference in weight of the primary component and the second, called in for comparison. In our previous example, Romeo's love affair provided a stable basis of fact even though the metaphor reduced its reality-character. In the passage from Eliot, the dove and the bomber are more equally weighted so that the reader, prevented from giving concreteness to the one component at the expense of the other, is driven to still further abstraction. The fiery carrier of love and hate as well as the setting in which its descent occurs are both reduced to a mere shadow of the reality situations, which compete on equal terms. Also, in many modern poems the description of the components becomes fragmentary and scant of concrete detail.

An inspection of worksheets will frequently show that such high degree of abstraction is obtained by a gradual abbreviation and condensation of an originally more concrete form. As an illustration we may compare the early draft of the Spender passage quoted above with the final printed version:

> By night I hold you, but by day
> I watch you weave the silk cocoon
> Of a son's, or a skater's, play:
> We have no meeting place
> Beneath that dancing, glassy surface:
> The outward figure of delight
> Creates no warm and sanguine image
> Answering my language.

The early simile kept the two reality-components of the original experience, the skater and the woman, clearly isolated. The final version fuses the two motifs to such a degree that the reality-content of the whole is reduced to a sequence of brief, heterogeneous glimpses. An interesting short circuit between the "silk" of the first component and the "weaving" of the second has introduced yet another reality-segment, the cocoon, thus pressing for further abstraction. The early motif of the dancer reappears, not instead of but together with the skater, and combines with "glassy surface" in a complicated image. The concreteness of "skater" is diminished through the introduction of a mysterious "son." In short, the intimate syntactic connection achieved through subject-predicate relationship, possessive genitive, etc., joins many elements of heterogeneous origin. This confines the experience of the reader forcibly to the physiognomic level, on which the various elements reveal their kinship and hence their capacity of merging in a common whole.*

The worksheets also contain cases in which metaphoric reality-elements are eliminated during the process of elaboration because they endanger the unity of the whole. Stephen Spender writes:

The spring like a sea of liquid flame catches the branches

and changes it into:

The spring like a spreading liquid flame hangs to the branches.

In addition to the idea of vastness, the "sea" carries powerful other qualities which would seem to be in discord with the physiognomic character of the whole. Probably the mutual annihilation of water and fire was not introduced intentionally but occurred as an accident. Hence "sea" was replaced by "spreading," a term whose contribution is limited to the one desired quality.

* Examples like this suggest that the study of worksheets will offer valuable clues to the better understanding of enigmatic modern poetry.

IV

Envoy. It may have occurred to the reader that the selection of the topics which have been discussed in this paper as well as the allotment of space in each case are largely subjective. This is inevitable particularly in a field of study so new that one author's bias is not sufficiently counterbalanced by the work of others.

Some pertinent subjects have not been treated at all. For instance I have not mentioned the interesting contributions which the Buffalo collection will be able to make to the acoustic aspects of poetry. The problem of the rhythmic structure of a line, a stanza, a poem, and its function as an interpreter of content will be greatly clarified by analyses of the changes which occur in the process of elaboration. In this connection it will be possible also to study the isomorphism of vowel and consonant structure on the one hand and the meaning to be conveyed on the other. These questions, which are of importance for the psychology of linguistic expression, have already attracted the attention of literary theorists, as shown for instance in M. R. Ridley's intensive study of Keats' craftsmanship.

Finally, there is one field for research which should be mentioned. The poetical effort can be described as a process in which a whole-structure tends to obtain its optimal state. Similar processes occur everywhere in the biological and psychological field, in the formation and functioning of organisms, of a social group, of a personality, as well as in the stages of thought which lead to a scientific theory. The worksheets of writers will give insight into the genesis and pathology of whole-structures in a particular field. A cursory inspection of the material shows that there are typical early stages of organization in which motifs appear which "belong" to the central theme of the poem but are not yet clarified as to the specific place and function they are to assume within the whole and with regard to other elements of the structure. One can observe them floating in the space of the poem, tentatively anchored here and there, changing their syntactic connection with other motifs, assuming a leading role at one moment and being demoted to the ranks in the next. The study of worksheets promises to contribute to the clarification of the widely used but undefined concept "simplicity." The final form of a work of art has simplicity, but not in the sense that it contains few elements, even though elimination of the superfluous is a part of the process. A good work of art is simple because it organizes its entire material in a transparent whole-structure, which defines the function of all parts, large compositional over-all features as well as minute details. Such simplicity is possible on any level of complexity. The struggle for simplicity is one against intricacy, disorder, summation of accidental elements, chaos. The gradual tightening of inner relations which leads to simplicity is exciting to watch. The process of organization consists not only in the pulling together of parts but also in the establishment of barriers, which segregate sub-wholes from each other. The visual arts offer material for comparison, for instance in the successive states of etchings. So may the sketchbooks of composers.

Probably, the opportunity to witness the poet's laboring for perfection will turn out to be the most valuable contribution of the worksheets. Accomplished works of art are always a little detached from us. Their faultlessness chills our admiration with a small dose of discouragement. They are the purest echo of ourselves, and we are told that they are of human origin; yet no bridge seems to lead to them from what we ourselves achieve. The Buffalo collection offers proof that even the good poems are made by man. The manuscripts show obstinate, incorruptible laboring for an aim, which is neither the selfishly desirable nor the diplomatically obtainable, but the absolute good. They are a demonstration of what man does when he is free and capable of using freedom for his own fulfillment. I can imagine that some poets may hesitate or even refuse to exhibit anything imperfect, mindful perhaps of the proverbial warning that one must never show a half-finished job to a fool. Undoubtedly, it is becoming for an artist to hold that nothing but his final word deserves publication. Yet, he ought to feel assured that, in addition to his work, he can offer an encouraging example of conduct by surrendering the testimony of uncompromising endeavor.

Squares and Oblongs

W. H. AUDEN

"We have made oblongs and stood them upon squares. This is our triumph; this is our consolation."

—VIRGINIA WOOLF

"A poet is someone who having nothing to do, finds something to do."

—THOREAU

"Maturity—to recover the seriousness one had as a child at play."

—NIETZSCHE

"He would like to be religious but remains a poet. Consequently, he is unhappily in love with God."

—KIERKEGAARD

There is nothing left of the sea but its sound,
Under the earth/ground the loud sea walks;
In a deathbed of orchards the boat dies down
And the anchor dives among hayricks,
                bait is drowned among

Down, down, down, under the ground,
Under the floating villages,
        Spins
Moves the moon-chained the and (water) wound
metropolis I listen,

                        nothing remains
Land, land, land, there is nothing left
Of the deep, famous sea but its speech
        stalking, famous
    It He pacing
And the anchor dives through the floors
of a church
                talking
Into its seven tombs

                talking
And into its seven tombs
The anchor dives through the floors of a
church

                pacing
Land, land, land, nothing remains
Of the stalking, famous sea but its speech,
And into its talking, seven tombs
The anchor dives through the floors of a church

Worksheet of "The Ballad of the Long-Legged Bait," by Dylan
Thomas. (See pages 178-9.)

THE MOST significant fact about the Buffalo collection of manuscripts is that it exists, because one cannot imagine the idea occurring to anyone before the twentieth century. Until recently the concern of critics and public alike was a reader's concern with the final published product, the questions of value they raised, readers' questions. "Is it good or bad? Why do I like it or dislike it?"

But the existence of this collection seems to me a sign—there are plenty of others—that, today, more and more people are coming to look at poetry, for instance, not primarily as readers but as actual or potential poets, to be raising therefore quite different questions. "How is poetry written? Could I write it? Is writing poetry a valuable occupation? Would I like being a poet?"

I hope I shall not be thought entirely irrelevant, therefore, if I leave to my fellow contributors to this symposium all discussion of the manuscripts themselves, and offer a few random subjective observations about the nature, pleasures, limits and dangers of the poetic vocation.

．　　．　　．　　．　　．　　．　　．

It is surely astonishing how many young people of both sexes, when asked what they want to be in life, give neither a sensible answer like "a lawyer, a farmer, an innkeeper," nor a romantic answer like "an explorer, a racing motorist, a missionary, President of the United States." No, an astonishing number reply "a writer," and by writing they mean—dreadful word—"creative" writing. Even if they say: "I want to go into journalism," this is only because they are under the illusion that in that profession they will be able to create. Even if their most genuine desire is really to make money, they will still make for some highly paid sub-literary pursuit like Advertising.

.   .   .   .

Among this host of would-be writers, the majority have no literary gift. This is not surprising in itself. A marked gift for anything is not very common. What *is* surprising is that such a high percentage of those without a marked talent for any particular profession should think of writing as the solution. One would expect that a certain percentage would imagine they had a talent for medicine, a certain percentage for engineering, and so on. But this is not the case. In our age, if a boy or a girl is untalented, the odds are in favor of their thinking they want to write.

.   .   .   .

When so many untalented people all express a wish to write, the public must be laboring under some strange misapprehensions as to the nature of literature. They must imagine, for example,

either (1) That writing requires no special talent but is something that any human being, by virtue of his humanity, can do if he tries.

or (2) That writing is the only occupation today in which one is free to do as one likes, the only one in modern society where one can act as an individual, not as a depersonalized cog in a machine.

(3) That writing—and this idea is, I think, particularly prevalent in regard to the writing of poetry—is a kind of religious technique, a way of learning to be happy and good.

In my opinion, the public is partially right as regards (2), namely in thinking that the writing of art is gratuitous, i.e.

play, but precisely because of this, their other two ideas must be wrong.

. . . .

St. Augustine was the first real psychologist for he was the first to see the basic fact about human nature, namely that the Natural Man hates nature, and that the only act which can really satisfy him is the *acte gratuite*. His ego resents every desire of his natural self for food, sex, pleasure, logical coherence, because desires are given not chosen, and his ego seeks constantly to assert its autonomy by doing something of which the requiredness is not given, that is to say, something which is completely arbitrary, a pure act of choice. The psychoanalyst can doubtless explain St. Augustine's robbing of the pear-tree in terms of natural desire, as, say, a symbolic copy of some forbidden sexual act, but this explanation, however true, misses the point which is the drive behind the symbolic transformation in consequence of which what in its original form was felt as a given desire now seems to the actor a matter of free and arbitrary choice.

Similarly, there are no doubt natural causes, perhaps very simple ones, behind the wish to write verses, but the chief satisfaction in the creative act is the feeling that it is quite gratuitous.

. . . .

In addition to wanting to feel free, man wants to feel important, and it is from the immediately given feelings with which he identifies himself that the natural man derives his sense of self-importance. In consequence he is in a dilemma, for the more he emancipates himself from given necessity, the more he loses his sense of importance and becomes a prey to anxiety.

That is why so many *actes gratuites* are, like that of St. Augustine, criminal acts. The freedom is asserted by disobeying a law of God or man which gives the importance. Nearly all crime is magic, an attempt to make free with necessities.

.   .   .   .

The alternative to criminal magic is the innocent game. Games are *actes gratuites* in which necessity is obeyed because the necessity here consists of rules chosen by the players. Games, therefore, are freer than crimes because the rule obeyed in the former is arbitrary while the rule disobeyed in the latter is not; at the same time, they are less important.

.   .   .   .

The rules of a game give it importance by making it difficult to play, a test of skill. In this, however, they betray that their importance is really frivolous, because it means that they are only important to those who have the physical or mental gifts to play them, and that is a matter of chance.

Granted that a game is innocent, the test of whether one should play it or not is simply whether one enjoys playing it or not, because the better one plays the more one enjoys it. A cripple may dream of being a star football player but he would feel miserable if he were actually compelled to play football.

Ask a talented surgeon why he is a surgeon and, if he is an honest man, he will not say: "Because I want to benefit suffering humanity"; he will say: "What a silly question. Because I love operating, of course." It is perfectly possible to imagine a surgeon who hated human beings at the same time that he saved their lives, because of the pleasure he took in exercising his gift.

.   .   .   .

The only serious possession of men is not their gifts but what they all possess equally, independent of fortune, namely their will, in other words, their love, and the only serious matter is what they love, themselves, or God and their neighbor. Life is not a game because one cannot say: "I will live if I turn out to be good at living." No, gifted or not, I must live. Those who cannot play a game can always be spectators, but no one can be a spectator of life; he must either live himself or hang himself. And in living well, i.e. in loving one's neighbor, the pleasure-pain criterion does not apply. If the Good Samaritan is asked why he rescued the man who fell among thieves, he may answer: "because I like doing good," but this answer will be a joking reproof to the interrogator for asking silly questions when he already knows the answer, which is that to love my neighbor as myself is an order and whether I enjoy obeying an order or not is irrelevant. If pleasure and pain were relevant, then the Good Samaritan would simply be more gifted at loving than the Levite, and the whole thing would be a game.

. . . .

To hear people talk, you would think that in their free time, i.e. when not engaged either in action or directed thinking, they were concerned with nothing but sex, prestige and money.

But the very readiness with which we frankly discuss such matters with each other is a sign that they are not our serious concern. Underneath them our serious day-dream carries on its repetitious querulous life, and it too has its manifest and latent content. What it actually says over and over again is: "Why doesn't my neighbor love me for myself?", but this is a code message which, decoded, reads: "I do not love my neighbor as myself and may God have mercy on my soul." About this, just because it is a serious matter. we quite rightly keep silent in public.

. . . .

An angel by direct descent, a German by alliance
Yours were the wonder-chords that made despair a science.

To witness an act of selfishness or hatred—say a man beating his wife—makes one angry or unhappy. To witness an untalented act like a clumsy man wrestling with a window-blind or a bad line of poetry makes one laugh (if no serious suffering is involved). Indeed there are few better ways of spending a hilarious evening than in recalling the worst lines in English poetry.

. . . .

The Greeks, being esthetes, regarded life as a game, i.e. as a test of inborn *areté*. The compensation for the chorus who could not play was to enjoy seeing the star players come one by one to a sticky end.

. . . .

There is a game called Cops and Robbers, but none called Saints and Sinners.

. . . .

Crossword puzzles, spelling bees, quizzes, questionnaires, games of knowledge. All knowledge is frivolous for the same reason that it is innocent, namely because it does not of itself move what is serious, the will. Only the will can will to make use of knowledge. As demagogues know only too well, knowledge itself is apt, if anything, to ensnare the mind in frivolous self-reflection and paralyze the will. How often is it true that the ignorant who do not know how to help their neighbor and the weak who lack the power to help him, nevertheless, are the ones who love him, while the learned and strong who could help him, do not because they no longer love him; on the contrary they use their knowledge and their power to rob and enslave him.

. . . .

The gulf between frivolity and seriousness, between choosing to obey the rules of a game which it does not matter whether you play or not, and choosing to obey the rules of life which you have to live whether you like it or not and where the rules are necessary for they do not cease to exist if you disobey them but operate within you to your destruction, this gulf is so infinite that all talk about children's games being a preparation for adult life is misleading twaddle.

A poet is, before anything else, a person who is passionately in love with language. Whether this love is a sign of his poetic gift or the gift itself—for falling in love is given not chosen—I don't know, but it is certainly the sign by which one recognizes whether a young man is potentially a poet or not.

"Why do you want to write poetry?" If the young man answers: "I have important things I want to say," then he is not a poet. If he answers: "I like hanging around words listening to what they say," then maybe he is going to be a poet.

As T. S. Eliot has said in one of his essays, the sign of promise in a young writer is not originality of idea or emotion, but technical competence. The subject matter of promising juvenilia is as a rule slight and unimportant, the style derivative, but this slight derivative thing is completely said.

In the first stages of his development, before he has found his distinctive style, the poet is, as it were, engaged to language and, like any young man who is courting, it is right and proper that he should play the chivalrous servant, carry parcels, submit to tests and humiliations, wait hours at street corners, and defer to his beloved's slightest whims, but once he has proved his love and been accepted, then it is another matter. Once he is married, he must be master in his own house and be responsible for their relationship.

. . . .

The poet is the father who begets the poem which the language bears. At first sight this would seem to give the poet too little to do and the language too much till one remembers that, as the husband, it is he, not the language, who is responsible for the success of their marriage which differs from natural marriage in that in this relationship there is no loveless lovemaking, no accidental pregnancies.

. . . .

Poets, like husbands, are good, bad and indifferent. Some are Victorian tyrants who treat language like a doormat, some are dreadfully hen-pecked, some bored, some unfaithful. For all of them, there are periods of tension, brawls, sulky silences, and, for many, divorce after a few passionate years.

. . . .

In the course of many centuries a few labor-saving devices have been introduced into the mental kitchen—alcohol, coffee, tobacco, benzedrine—but these mechanisms are very crude, liable to injure the cook, and constantly breaking down. Writing poetry in the twentieth century A.D. is pretty much the same as it was in the twentieth century B.C.: nearly everything has still to be done by hand.

. . . .

Rhymes, meters, stanza-forms, etc., are like servants. If the master is just enough to win their affection and firm enough to command their respect, the result is an orderly happy household. If he is too tyrannical, they give notice; if he lacks authority, they become slovenly, impertinent, drunken and dishonest.

The poet who writes "free" verse is like Robinson Crusoe on his desert island: he must do all his cooking, laundry, darning, etc., for himself. In a few exceptional cases this manly independence produces something original and impressive, but as a rule the result is squalor—empty bottles on the unswept floor and dirty sheets on the unmade bed.

. . . . . .

Milton's intuition in his *Ode on the Nativity* gives the lie to his personal over-estimation of the poet's importance. If the Fall made man conscious of the difference between good and evil, then the Incarnation made him conscious of the difference between seriousness and frivolity and exorcised the world. Before that, one might say that only children, i.e. those in whom the consciousness of good and evil was not yet fully developed, could play games. The adult had to take frivolity seriously, i.e. turn games into magic, and in consequence could never wholeheartedly enjoy them because necessarily he was always anxious as to whether the magic would work this time.

. . . .

Two theories of poetry. Poetry as a magical means for inducing desirable emotions and repelling undesirable emotions in oneself and others, or Poetry as a game of knowledge, a bringing to consciousness, by naming them, of emotions and their hidden relationships.

The first view was held by the Greeks, and is now held by MGM, Agit-Prop, and the collective public of the world. They are wrong.

. . . . . .

Being ignorant of the difference between seriousness and frivolity, the Greeks confused art with religion. In spite of this, they produced great works of art. This was possible because in reality, like all pagans, they were frivolous people who took nothing seriously. Their religion was just a camp.

But we, whether Christians or not, cannot escape our consciousness of what is serious and what is not. Consequently, if we try to treat art as magic, we produce, not great works of art, but only dishonest and insufferably earnest and boring Agit-Prop for Christianity, Communism, Free Enterprise or what have you.

.   .   .   .

How can I know what I think till I see what I say? A poet writes "The chestnut's comfortable root" and then changes this to "The chestnut's customary root." In this alteration there is no question of replacing one emotion by another, or of strengthening an emotion, but of discovering what the emotion is. The emotion is unchanged, but waiting to be identified like a telephone number one cannot remember. "8357. No, that's not it. 8557, 8457, no, it's on the tip of my tongue, wait a moment, I've got it, 8657. That's it."

.   .   .   .

There are events which arouse such simple and obvious emotions that an AP cable or a photograph in *Life* magazine are enough and poetic comment is impossible. If one reads through the mass of versified trash inspired, for instance, by the Lidice Massacre, one cannot avoid the conclusion that what was really bothering the versifiers was a feeling of guilt at not feeling horrorstruck enough. Could a good poem have been written on such a subject? Possibly. One that revealed this lack of feeling, that told how when he read the news, the poet, like you and I, dear reader, went on thinking about his fame or his lunch, and how glad he was that he was not one of the victims.

.   .   .   .

Christianity knows of only one predestined life like the lives of the mythical heroes of Greek tragedy and this life is (a) not a myth, (b) not a tragedy. Further, esthetic values have nothing to do with its ritual representation; whether the Mass is well or badly sung is irrelevant.

.   .   .   .

If I understand what Aristotle means when he speaks of catharsis, I can only say he is wrong. It is an effect produced, not by works of art, but by bull-fights, professional football matches, bad movies and, in those who can stand that sort of thing, monster rallies at which ten thousand girl guides form themselves into the national flag.

.   .   .   .

If art were magic, then love lyrics would be love charms which made the Cruel Fair give one her latch key. In that case a magnum of champagne would be more artistic than a sonnet.

.   .   .   .

The girl whose boy-friend starts writing her love poems should be on her guard. Perhaps he really does love her, but one thing is certain: while he was writing his poems he was not thinking of her but of his own feelings about her, and that is suspicious. Let her remember St. Augustine's confession of his feelings after the death of someone he loved very much: "I would rather have been deprived of my friend than of my grief."

.   .   .   .

Everyone in his heart of hearts agrees with Baudelaire: "To be a useful person has always seemed to me something particularly horrible," for, subjectively, to be useful means to be doing not what one wants to do, but what someone else insists on one's doing. But at the same time, everyone is ashamed to admit in public that he is useless. Thus if a poet gets into conversation with a stranger in a railway coach and the latter asks him: "What is your job?", he will think quickly and say: "A schoolteacher, a beekeeper, a bootlegger," because to tell the truth would cause an incredulous and embarrassing silence.

. . . .

The day of the Master's study with its vast mahogany desk on which the blotting paper is changed every day, its busts of Daunty, Gouty and Shopkeeper, its walls lined with indexed bookshelves, one of which is reserved for calf-bound copies of the Master's own works, is over for ever. From now on the poet will be lucky if he can have the general living room to himself for a few hours or a corner of the kitchen table on which to keep his papers. The soft carpets, the big desks, will all be reserved by the Management for the whopping liars.

. . . .

Over too, the day of the salon and the café, the select group of enthusiastic rebels. No more movements. No more manifestoes. Every poet stands alone. This does not mean that he sulks mysteriously in a corner by himself; on the contrary he may, perhaps, lead a more social life than before, but as a neighbor like his neighbors, not as a poet. Where his gift is concerned, he stands alone and joins nobody, least of all his contemporary brother poets.

. . . .

The ideal audience the poet imagines consists of the beautiful who go to bed with him, the powerful who invite him to dinner and tell him secrets of state, and his fellow-poets. The actual audience he gets consists of myopic schoolteachers, pimply young men who eat in cafeterias, and his fellow-poets. This means that, in fact, he writes for his fellow-poets.

. . . .

Happy the lot of the pure mathematician. He is judged solely by his peers and the standard is so high that no colleague can ever win a reputation he does not deserve. No cashier writes articles in the Sunday *Times* complaining about the incomprehensibility of Modern Mathematics and comparing it unfavorably with the good old days when mathematicians were content to paper irregularly shaped rooms or fill bath-tubs with the waste-pipe open. Better still, since engineers and physicists have occasionally been able to put his equations to destructive use, he is even given a chair in a State University.

. . . .

The poet is capable of every form of conceit but that of the social worker:—"We are all here on earth to help others; what on earth the others are here for I don't know."

. . . . . .

How glad I am that the silliest remark ever made about poets, "the unacknowledged legislators of the world," was made by a poet whose work I detest. Sounds more like the secret police to me.

. . . .

The Prophet says to men: "Thus saith the Lord."
The Poet says firstly to God: "Lord, do I mean what I say?" and secondly to men: "Do you mean what I mean?"
Agit-Prop says to men: "You mean what I say and to hell with the Lord who, even if he exists, is rotten with liberalism anyway."

. . . .

From now on the only popular art will be comic art, like Groucho Marx or Li'l Abner, and this will be unpopular with the Management. Whatever their differences, highbrows and lowbrows have a common enemy, The Law (the Divine as well as the secular), and it is the Law which it cannot alter which is the subject of all comic art. What is not comic will either be highbrow art, or popular or official magic.

. . . .

It is a sobering experience for any poet to read the last page of the Book Section of the Sunday *Times* where correspondents seek to identify poems which have meant much to them. He is forced to realize that it is not his work, not even the work of Dante or Shakespeare, that most people treasure as magic talismans in times of trouble, but grotesquely bad verses written by maiden ladies in local newspapers; that millions in their bereavements, heartbreaks, agonies, depressions, have been comforted and perhaps saved from despair by appalling trash while poetry stood helplessly and incompetently by.

. . . .

The frightful falsehood which obsessed the Greeks and Romans and for which mankind has suffered ever since, was that government is a similar activity to art, that human beings are a medium like language out of which the gifted politician creates a good society as the gifted poet creates a good poem.

. . . .

A society which really was like a poem and embodied all the esthetic values of beauty, order, economy, subordination of detail to the whole effect, would be a nightmare of horror, based on selective breeding, extermination of the physically or mentally unfit, absolute obedience to its Director, and a large slave class kept out of sight in cellars.

. . . .

The poet writes:

> The mast-high anchor dives through a cleft

changes it to

> The anchor dives through closing paths

then to

> The anchor dives among hayricks

finally to

> The anchor dives through the floors of a church.

The cleft and the closing paths have been liquidated and the hayricks deported to another stanza.

There's Creative Politics and Scientific Government for you.

.   .   .   .

All poets adore explosions, thunderstorms, tornadoes, conflagrations, ruins, scenes of spectacular carnage. The poetic imagination is therefore not at all a desirable quality in a chief of state.

.   .   .   .

The democratic idea that anyone should be able to become president is right. For to talk of the profession of politics or a gifted politician ought to be nonsense. A good politician ought to mean someone who loves his neighbor and, with God's help, anyone can do that if he choose.

.   .   .   .

If God were a poet or took poetry seriously (or science too for that matter), he would never have given man free will.

.   .   .   .

The old superstition that it is dangerous to love a poet is perhaps not without some foundation. Given the opportunity, a poet is perhaps more tempted than others to drop his old innocent game of playing God with words, and take up that much more exciting but forbidden game of creating a human being, that game which starts off with such terrific gusto but always ends sooner or later in white faces and a fatal accident.

.   .   .   .

His life was like a poem. If so, he was a very great scoundrel who said to himself early in life: "I will explore every

possibility of sinning and then repent on my death-bed."
Faust? Exactly. Marlowe was not as intelligent as Goethe but
he had more common sense. At least he knew that Faust went
to hell. Faust is damned, not because he has sinned, but because he made a pact with the Devil, that is, like a poet he
planned a life of sin beforehand.

    .   .   .   .

The low-brow says: "I don't like poetry. It requires too
much effort to understand and I'm afraid that if I learnt
exactly what I feel, it would make me most uncomfortable."
He is in the wrong, of course, but not so much in the wrong
as the highbrow whose gifts make the effort to understand
very little and who, having learned what he feels, is not at
all uncomfortable, only interested.

    .   .   .   .

Orpheus who moved stones is the archetype, not of the
poet, but of Goebbels. The archetype, not of the poet as such,
but of the poet who loses his soul for poetry, is Narcissus.

    .   .   .   .

Being esthetes, the Greeks were naive psychologists. Narcissus does not fall in love with his reflection because it is
beautiful but because it is like himself. In a later version of
the myth, it is a hydrocephalic idiot who gazes entranced into
the pool, saying: "On me it looks good." In another, still
more sophisticated version, Narcissus is neither beautiful nor
ugly but as completely average as a Thurber husband, and
instead of addressing his image with the declarative "I love
you," he puts to it over and over again the same question,
"Haven't we met before someplace?"

    .   .   .   .

The present state of the world is so miserable and degraded
that if anyone were to say to the poet: "For God's sake, stop
humming and put the kettle on or fetch bandages. The pa-

tient's dying," I do not know how he could justifiably refuse. (There is, of course, an inner voice which says exactly this to most of us, and our only reply is to pretend to be extremely hard of hearing.) But no one says this. The self-appointed unqualified Nurse says: "Stop humming this instant and sing the Patient a song which will make him fall in love with me. In return I'll give you extra ration-cards and a passport"; and the poor Patient in his delirium cries: "Please stop humming and sing me a song which will make me believe I am free from pain and perfectly well. In return I'll give you a penthouse apartment in New York and a ranch in Arizona."

To such requests and to the bribes that go with them, the poet can only pray that he will always have the courage to stick out his tongue, say, like Olaf the conscientious objector in Cummings' poem,—"There is some s. I will not eat,"— and go on humming quietly to himself.

Index